LIVING PROOF

From Foster Care to the White House and the NBA

Lucas Daniel Boyce

Life Lessons for Success, Leadership and Character

Published by Advantage, Charleston, South Carolina.
Member of Advantage Media Group.

ADVANTAGE is a registered trademark and the Advantage colophon is a trademark of Advantage Media Group, Inc.

Printed in the United States of America.

ISBN: 978-1-59932-257-5
LCCN: 2010918954

This publication is designed to provide accurate and authoritative information in regard to the subject matter covered. It is sold with the understanding that the publisher is not engaged in rendering legal, accounting, or other professional services. If legal advice or other expert assistance is required, the services of a competent professional person should be sought.

Tree Neutral

Advantage Media Group is proud to be a part of the Tree Neutral™ program. Tree Neutral offsets the number of trees consumed in the production and printing of this book by taking proactive steps such as planting trees in direct proportion to the number of trees used to print books. To learn more about Tree Neutral, please visit www.treeneutral.com. To learn more about Advantage's commitment to being a responsible steward of the environment, please visit www.advantagefamily.com/green

Advantage Media Group is a leading publisher of business, motivation, and self-help authors. Do you have a manuscript or book idea that you would like to have considered for publication? Please visit www.amgbook.com or call 1.866.775.1696

DEDICATION

✧✧

Mom, your life example, sacrifice, counsel and courage are an inspiration to not only me but to lives you'll never know you've touched. Thank you for taking me in and adopting me into your family. I will never forget your incredible gift of love and it is the great honor of my life to be your son.

—Lucas Daniel

CONTENTS

ACKNOWLEDGMENTS

I want to thank former President George W. Bush. Were it not for your incredible kindness to a random kid you met during a photo opportunity, none of my life dreams would have been possible.

I also want to thank an amazing editor and friend Crystal Whiteaker along with design guru Christina Thorpe and confidants Dan Dugger, Paris Dennard and Jeramie Anderson. Their contributions of time, advice and hard work were invaluable to this manuscript's development.

John and Lori Perry mentored me with this very simple phrase, "you don't get anything if you don't ask." I thank you both for allowing me into your home and instilling in me a seed of desire.

My colleagues from the Bush-Cheney 2004 Presidential Campaign and the White House are too many to mention individually but I'm indebted to them all, especially my dear friends who I served with in the Office of Public Liaison and Political Affairs. Ed Moy and Andrea McDaniel, thank you for choosing me as your White House Intern. Steve Schmidt, thank you for taking me under your wing. Rhonda Keenum, thank you for giving me a second chance. Jason Recher and John Myers made flying on Air Force One possible. And Kevin Sullivan's friendship made the transition from the White House to the NBA a reality.

Working for an NBA franchise would never have been possible were it not for Joel Glass, Lorisse Garcia, Otis Smith, Alex Martins, Linda Landman Gonzalez, and Audra Hollifield. Pat Williams told me that I should capture my story in writing and share it with others. This book was born with your encouragement.

To all my friends, thank you for believing in me.

INTRODUCTION

Some men see things as they are... and ask why?
Others dream things that can be... and ask why not?
—Nobel Laureate George Bernard Shaw

Eyewitness to Grace

May 29, 2008

Thursday Morning

Aboard Air Force One

It was the last leg of a three-day cross-country trip that took us through New Mexico, Arizona, Utah and Colorado. As we prepared to touch down at New Century Airport in Olathe, Kansas, I peered out the window just off the right wing of Air Force One, deep in reflection.

The last few days were a presidential whirlwind: visits to small businesses, statements on the economy, a commencement address to the 2008 graduating class of the U.S. Air Force Academy – and a few fundraisers peppered amidst the official events. As an associate director for the Political Affairs office, I oversaw political activity and event planning for the president in ten states spread throughout the Mid and Southwest. From the towering St. Louis Arch in Missouri to the sprawling vineyards of California's Napa Valley, it was my good fortune to serve the country. And while it was a tremendous amount of work, any sense of fatigue was outweighed by the overwhelming sense of gratitude I felt for the unique and rare privilege to work for and travel with the president of the United States. A river of polarizing, contradictory emotions coursed through me.

I thought of the first few decades of my life and relived the challenges caused by choices I had no control over. Twenty-nine years prior, I was prematurely born as the undesirable byproduct of a 19-year-old drug addict who abused alcohol. My birth mother, a young black teenager with unlimited potential and intelligence, got caught up with the wrong crowd and went down a path that changed her life forever. Put bluntly, my birth mother was a drug addict, who fed her appetite for drugs and thirst for booze by turning tricks on the streets of Kansas City, Missouri. Sometimes the tricks led to money that was used for drugs. Other times, the tricks just led to drugs. At the end of the day, after the drugs and tricks and whatever else was involved, the result was me.

Looking out the window of Air Force One, I thought of how life began for me as an orphan labeled an illegitimate mistake with failure as my birthright, and whispered a brief prayer. *"Thank you."* Flipping back through the pages of time I accessed the part of my memory where some of my most cherished, vivid moments were stored: three years spent in foster care; struggling with developmental delays; being adopted by white parents; growing up in a bi-cultural household. Tears welled up and my eyes began to mist.

As I reviewed nearly 30 years of memories and tried to reconcile past challenges with being on Air Force One, I asked myself, *Whoever would have believed or imagined that the illegitimate kindergarten-flunking son of a 19-year-old drug and alcohol abusing crack-whore would ever amount to anything — much less fly with the president aboard Air Force One?* As I reflected on God's grace and the unmerited favor that had brought me this far, thoughts turned to one person in particular who made this daunting feat possible. Brought to her doorstep by way of grace, that one special person was waiting on the tarmac in Kansas with a big hug and a smile.

Our nation is on a continuous search for heroes and leaders of supernatural ability. With the leader of our country receiving national security briefings in his presidential suite at the front of the plane, I asked myself a question that I had pondered several times before: *what really makes someone a great leader, a hero? What qualities must one possess to reach the highest pedestal of our admiration and become the apple of our eye?* Is it the number of points they score in a basketball game or how many strokes below par they golf? Is it the ability to captivate audiences and inspire nations to come together and meet the challenges of our time? Is it walking on the moon or finding the cure for all cancers? These characteristics, though very much the attributes of heroes we have heard of – or yet hope to know – are still the talents of such a small percentage of the population that it is unlikely we will ever see them in someone we know.

Or will we?

Authentic heroes quietly cross our paths each day, unrecognized, because they are not defined or classified conventionally – rather, they can be identified by their core characteristics. Their contributions are far greater and have far more impact than we realize. They go about their daily lives unnoticed, and, sadly, more often than not, unappreciated. Yet, these heroes, these testaments to true leadership, are more real than any professional sports superstar or astronaut. They are the genuine witnesses of moral virtue. They are more influential than any politician, statesmen, billionaire or actor. Yet they fly under the radar, with their bright red heroic capes of selfless sacrifice. Through their discipline, love, encouragement and unwavering determination we are inspired to reach for something more than we are. They lead us to invest in the promise of a future that is already laid out if we only have the courage to think big, step outside ourselves and leave fear by the side of the road.

I am proud to be the son of a true American hero. Dorothy doesn't have an oversized personality and she wasn't born on the planet Krypton, but to me, she can still fly. With a small frame, standing five feet seven inches, my Irish-born, adoptive mother is a woman of steel. She reminds me of that Energizer Bunny in those Energizer battery commercials. She keeps going and going and going, no matter what lies ahead. Behind her sunny and friendly disposition and quick wit is a woman who possesses a wealth of knowledge and an ever-growing faith that has been forged in the fires of life. There are some people who succumb to the flames, their lives made ash heaps because of the senseless and insensitive things humans do to each other sometimes. Not Mom. She's like the three Hebrew boys in the Old Testament who stood up for what they believed in, would not go with the crowd, and were thrown into an old-time crematory "fiery furnace" as a result. Chapter three in the book of Daniel tells us King Nebuchadnezzar looked into the fire expecting the worst but witnessed something all-together different. The king not only saw the three Hebrew boys alive and well. He saw a fourth person in the fire with them and the fourth looked like the Son of God, the king said. Mom's faith has brought her a mighty long way and through many fires. When things have been the hottest, I'm convinced she's so incredibly strong because of her faith and that other person in the fire.

I never got to know my birth mother and my biological father remains a mystery. I haven't seen my biological mother since I was almost three years old and she signed the document that paved the way for my adoption. But I'm thankful for an adopted mom, regardless of her skin color, who believed in me. Dorothy Lee didn't cast me aside as another tragic statistic, indicative of hard life on the streets.

Mom believed that I was created for something greater and wouldn't yield to a society that yawns at failure and quickly casts it aside. Mom's life is the purest testament to decency, honor and integrity that I've ever seen; her virtues those that any would-be leader or hero should aspire to. Mom would never, in a million years, define herself in this way. But I, and the many others who benefited from the full measure of her devotion, can testify on her behalf. I know, without a doubt, were it not for her example of leadership and constant sacrifice, I would never have dreamed it possible to work for the president of the United States. If asked whether super heroes exist in a world filled with sad stories, disaster and disappointments, I, along with my seven sisters and five brothers, can testify without reservation; "Yes, they do!"

Thursday, May 29, 2008 wasn't "just another day at the office" for me, but an important anniversary and life milestone. Twenty-nine years earlier, as a 10-day-old premature infant, finally big enough to be released from the hospital and weighing only 4.2 pounds, I was brought to Dorothy as a foster care child by the Division of Family Services (DFS). Since that time, May 29 serves as a second birthday for me because it was the day I truly arrived at home and began my life. And 29 years to the day that I was brought to her, my mother, Dorothy and my father, Larry watched Air Force One touch-down at a small airport in Kansas with their son aboard. To make the day even more special, our pilot had a surprise in store for them. He had agreed to give my parents a VIP tour of one of the most magnificent planes on earth.

I asked a friend of mine who was staying on board while I attended our scheduled event to point out to my mom where I sat. Knowing that she would pass by my seat, I quickly wrote a brief note:

Mom, I love you and thank you for everything you've done for me. I hope you and Dad enjoy the tour! —Lucas

New Century Airport in Olathe, Kansas Approximately 1:00 PM

When Air Force One rolled to a stop, I deplaned at the tail end with the rest of the junior staff and press. The sky was clear, and with it nearing one o'clock in the afternoon, the cement on the tarmac was quite warm; it was obvious that the cool air of spring was giving way to the humid heat of summer. I anxiously scanned the waiting crowd, looking for that familiar face, until I noticed Mom waving her arms excitedly. She was easy to spot, especially since she was the only one jumping up and down, an obvious annoyance to the Secret Service agents who were posted there.

She was beaming from ear to ear, prompting a smile to creep across my own face as well. The thought flashed, *My hero.*

A little concerned by her obvious animation, the Secret Service agent tried to gain control. "Excuse me Miss… Miss! Please stay in one spot. The plane is landing. You can't keep running back and forth."

Mom didn't want to miss seeing me deplane. She was normally a very soft-spoken individual and not one for public disturbance or disobedience to authority. My mom saw the agent's mouth moving but in her excitement pretended not to hear his rebuke. Never mind the crisp black suit, stern look, dark Ray Ban sunglasses, an earpiece and standard issue Sig Sauer 228 semiautomatic pistol at his side! "I have to get a good photo," she tried to reason with him. "My son is on the plane!"

She could hardly contain her excitement and to be honest, neither could I! I walked across the tarmac to the barricade and gave her and my dad a big hug. I told her and my stepfather I loved them and to enjoy the tour. Then I scurried off to a 15-passenger van in the waiting motorcade before I got left behind.

A few hours later when the presidential entourage returned to the airport for the two-and-a-half hour flight back to Washington D.C., a white piece of paper caught my eye as I took my seat. My mom had returned the favor and had written a reply.

Dear Lucas, waiting to board for this tour, I thought of 'our' life – your life – and it's more than humbling, isn't it? Thank you for giving us this day! Thank you for your good, sharing life. We love you so much!
—Mom & Dad. And I miss you.

> *When grace meets hard work and opportunity, anything can happen.*

As I read the note, my eyes filled with tears again. I could only imagine where I would be without the grace of my God and the adoptive mother He divinely appointed me to be with. Flying aboard Air Force One, serving at the White House, or accomplishing any of the other life goals that were still to come would not have been possible without Mom's life intermingling with my own. As a result, I'm very cognizant of the fact that when grace meets hard work and opportunity, anything can happen. I'm also keenly aware that these dreams were not achieved by my strength alone, or my ability, but by that which God has given.

I believe that if you want to be the greatest, the leader; you must first be willing to be the servant of all. While this is not an original philosophy, I witnessed this belief system first hand in the way my mother served and led our family of 11 and later 15. My mother's unfailing desire to give others a life of quality and meaning puts her on the level of our superstars and greatest heroes.

My hope is that I can encourage people with her example, by sharing what it has meant for me and for so many others. And maybe, just maybe, I can enable others to pursue their goals with a sense of purpose and buy into the fact that it doesn't matter where we start in life. What matters most is where we're going and the opportunity each of us has to shape our own destiny.

〰〰〰〰〰〰〰〰〰〰〰〰〰〰〰〰〰〰〰〰〰

CHAPTER ONE

A MOTHER'S VISION

Oh lord you have searched me and you have known me.
For you created my inmost being;
You knit me together in my mothers' womb
I Praise you because I am fearfully and wonderfully made;
Your works are wonderful, I know that full well.
—Psalms 139: 1, 13—14, New International Version (NIV)

Mom's Story

Dorothy, or "Dot," as friends and family call her, had a life-defining moment when she was nine years old. Her parents were west Texas farm folks who moved to southern California when Dot was about three years old. They settled in a diverse community in what Dot still considers one of the most beautiful towns, Redlands, California, in the world. Her dad worked as a field manager for an orange packing house. Her mom did a variety of different jobs – everything from front-line employee at the orange packing house, to house keeper for the upscale folks on Sunset Drive to selling hosiery or children's clothing at the local department store. She even did odd jobs like ironing the neighbor's clothes to earn enough money to make ends meet. She was also the mom to five children in a time when clothes were still washed in a wringer washer on Monday, hung outside to dry, brought in to be sprinkled down with water and rolled into a plastic bag, then ironed on Tuesday. Dot's mom had plenty on her plate, with no other family members within a thousand miles. The local church family and the values of the community where Dot's family lived served as a critical model for the principles that shaped her life decisions – the difference between right and wrong and what was most important.

Outside of immediate family and church friends, one person in particular helped form Dot's world view: her fourth grade teacher. It wasn't anything she taught – unless you wonder why Mom can still dance a mean "La Cucaraja" – but how she treated every student. Miss Marthalie Ann Chesnutt loved every child in the class. She made it a loving, giving, and wonderful place to learn. Mom has never had the desire to attend a class reunion, but if it were for THAT fourth grade class, she would go in a New York minute! All of her good school memories are rooted in that class and that teacher. Simply put; Mom genuinely felt her love and it had an impact on her life that remains to this day. It was during that school year, 1952-1953, that she realized that one didn't have to be a blood relative to love you. There didn't even have to be a reason – you could just be loved because you were you and there was something about that very fact that made you acceptable. Nothing else was needed. Mom's heart soared with that simple realization that she could be loved; and she realized she wanted all children to feel exactly what she felt. No matter who they were, or what color or gender. When Dot experienced unconditional love she realized that's what she wanted for everyone and planned then as a nine-year-old little girl, to someday be in a position where she could love children, as many as she could gather around her, just like Miss Chesnutt! Mom always figured that meant that she would become a teacher. That's not what happened exactly. She describes it this way:

> *It turns out that I am exceedingly shy; horribly, awfully, and completely shy. Once I realized what taking college classes would involve, I mean, I'd have to take a SPEECH class! Teaching just sort of faded away as a way to fulfill my dream.*

Mom did go off to a small school to become a nurse. And though she didn't complete the program, she took some insightful classes on human behavior, growth and development and met young girls – classmates – who came from all over the country and taught her wonderful lessons on acceptance and tolerance. In addition, one of those girls, LaDon Piepegerdes, became part of our family and is our "Aunt Donnie" for life!

Becoming a Foster Care Parent

Eventually Mom married and had four children. She had a sixth grade classmate in foster care, thus acquainting her with the family services system. She would always tell her first husband that someday she wanted to be a foster parent, but not until they bought a home, because she never wanted to ask a child who had been uprooted to have to move yet again. "The least I could do would be to provide a permanent place," she says.

In 1974, the family moved to Independence, MO. On their first Sunday at church Mom spotted a woman who was a foster mother and talked with her; what had been an idea or desire 20 years prior now began to take a serious form. They bought a turn-of-the–century farmhouse with three bedrooms and one bathroom. Their youngest child, Bo, turned three years old, and "it was time." Within a year ten children were living in the home. And that's all she wanted – to provide a secure, warm, accepting place for those children who were having difficult times. She wanted the children to know that there was a place where they were accepted and loved, where they were "good enough" just as they were. She wanted them to have what her fourth grade teacher Miss Chesnutt had given her. She knew the children weren't "hers" and she had no desire to take possession of them in any way. Many people would ask Dorothy, "Oh, how can you let them go?" "How could I not?" She would quickly reply.

It was Dorothy's belief that her primary task was to love her foster children with all her heart. Her mission centered on this core value: not to let them miss the most important thing this world owes them -to be planned for, to be wanted, to be loved. The fact that their birth parents couldn't provide it at that time meant she must bridge the gap and that's precisely what she did. She was never a foster child so she can't really tell you what the foster children's take on her approach was. What Mom was able to glean, however, was that just because she loved her children, wanted them and planned for them in her life, it did not necessarily mean that they would reciprocate in kind. After all, she reasoned they planned to be with their birth parents; and this stranger, Dorothy, was definitely not something they planned on. It was not required that the feelings of the foster children be the same as hers, and she was undeterred from her mission.

One day a caseworker brought a child to my mom who would never be able to return to her birth parents. She had some curious growth problems and was diagnosed with developmental delay. In time it became obvious that this little girl wouldn't be going to an adoptive home. Mom's heart melted. "I knew where she was accepted, wanted, loved and needed." Finally, the caseworker gave permission for Mom to apply to adopt this bundle of joy in need and the court granted the request! Mom recalls the judges' advice and counsel vividly:

> *We [as adoptive parents] were advised and reminded that this child now had all the legal rights in our family of any birth child. That was music to my ears.*

But the *wisest* thing said that day was rather 'harumphed' in a most judge-like way: "She won't always be little and cute, you know."

However, the most important fact of our lives remained: we were now legal and were the same as birth children and Mom wanted to be sure we never forgot this. More often than not, we would endure the jeering and snickering of children who did not understand. We were referred to as Mom's 'other children' or 'foster children,' never afforded the acknowledgement that we were just her children. Period. Mom strongly believes that "Nothing separates birth parents from adoptive ones except the prejudice or ignorance of other people." One story often retold in our family circle certainly describes the experience of any child living in that circumstance. At around nine years old, one of my mom's biological children was walking alongside one of my adopted sisters at school when a student approached her and asked her if that was "a real sister." In her most indignant "What are you crazy?" voice the sister replied, "Of course she's real. What da ya think? We're *cu-cum-bers*?!"

For 15 years, about 40 children came and went from Dot's house.

Mom worked with nearly 200 caseworkers during her time as a foster parent, due to the extremely high turnover in the social work field. Sometimes she provided a weekend "safe house," while other times it was for very long-term care, the longest being seven years.

The old farmhouse was renovated to accommodate the influx of children. With the addition of 2,800 square feet and some specific modifications she met the requirements of the state of Missouri to become a Foster Family Group Home. That meant extra inspections, classes, and anything else the State of Missouri needed. After the renovation, Mom had no fewer than eight non-birth children in her home at all times and was licensed for a maximum of 12 children. There were a couple of occasions when the number of children went to 15 for the occasional short-term emergency situations, which the license covered.

Adopting the Un-Adoptable

It was the role of foster parent that led my mother into adoption. She was never barren, never went to an agency, or to the Division of Family Services to petition approval. It was an unlikely path that led her to become an adoptive parent. Because she knew some of her adoptive children ahead of time, Mom didn't always have the typical experience most adoptive parents go through when deciding to enter the process. When the initial interview took place before being accepted as foster parents, the specific comment was made: "Now, you don't want to adopt? If you want to adopt you need to do something else or apply with an adoption agency. "Oh no," came the innocent reply, "we don't want to adopt. We want to be foster care parents."

Only once did the Division of Family Services call Dorothy specifically to ask her to adopt a child who was badly in need of a permanent home. It was after she had adopted me and actually took place outside the courtroom just after my adoption! The conversation began with, "Now that you are integrated and have a multicultural family..." He was eight years old and suffered from fetal alcohol effect (FAE). FAE is one of many complications that can affect a child who has been exposed to alcohol in the womb. Another child, Timothy, came to our home on his 16th birthday. My mother was told Tim didn't want parents and would only stay for a weekend while his caseworker found another place for him.

For my mother's part she was getting pretty burned out. It had been a trying year, as she had become a divorcee. The trials of life had piled up pretty high, even for Mom. Fresh off a divorce and thrown into the fire of single mommy-hood, she didn't feel particularly motivated to take on yet another teen. All of which was a set-up for A MATCH MADE IN HEAVEN! When he walked in the front door, Mom and Tim both knew he was home.

He never went to the residential home, but stayed and exasperated and delighted Mom for the rest of his life. He knew and understood Mom's heart and was obviously a key piece we had been waiting for. Mom knew Tim made our family more complete.

For Dorothy, adopting older children was always an important and worthwhile endeavor. She knew the lives of her adopted children had been very different from her own. She had been raised by two able parents and enjoyed a "normal" upbringing; she planned, dreamed, went to work, led a life of faith and had a future. So in adopting older children she often felt she was merely offering them a new start and a chance to take advantage of the types of choices she had benefited from, of which the most enduring was: accepting someone else's acceptance of you. The children that came to her had experienced a variety of circumstances, which, in some cases, left them emotionally and psychologically scarred. Mom offered an experience that focused on education, family, and friends; and for however long they were with her… peace. Her children could not be intimidated by what she had to offer, for there were few things she could offer them in terms of finances or worldly possession, but she hoped they knew they could have more choices in life.

Mom didn't expect an environment of love between herself and her foster children in the traditional sense; but rather she required an attitude of ever-evolving friendship. She knew that the needs of these children were very different from the needs of a newborn. She had one adopted son who was in so much need that when the family went to court she silently asked herself, *What if he murders someone? If he is ever accused of murder, could I stand beside him and go through the judicial process with him?* Fortunately, she's not had to find out the answer to that question, but she has accompanied him to court facing lesser charges. In adopting older children, she accepted that the challenges of upbringing were going to be different and perhaps unpleasant to bear at times.

One of the things Mom has always said in adopting older children is that she was "providing the child with someone to sit on his or her side of the church when they got married." Adopting older children cannot be any more demanding than traditional parenthood in her view. Mom always held the belief that "It is easy to think of older child placement as parenthood in a 'fast forward' position. So many parts of their lives have gone by, but still so much remains. And there are many significant events that must still unfold; establishing themselves as adults, graduation, birthday milestones, and marriage. As parents we can take part in all of it, the same as any parent."

Hindsight is 20/20, but in Mom's case it wouldn't do much good, for if Mom had to do it again, she wouldn't hesitate to adopt older children. Of the older children Mom adopted, Tim has passed away, and another remains so out of touch with reality that Mom never knows when she is going to hear from him. Another called her one day and said, "I found my real mom so I don't need you anymore." However, when she knows where to find him, she still takes him a loaf of her carrot bread at Christmas time.

Mom's only wish now is, "That I hadn't run out of gas for the future!" Dot still wishes she could provide a safe haven for what the Bible calls "the least of these" and adopt those that need a home; someplace where they know that they are accepted.

Mom still recalls the times when she had to do seven loads of laundry a day to keep from falling behind, overwhelmed by the mountains of linen, lights, darks and Sunday bests. If you can believe it, Mom misses needing five hours a day just to get the cooking done! She also misses the sense of hope in thinking that *If I could just hang in there, who knows what this little kid might decide for himself.* She misses when we were all kids and longs for days that in the moment were very hard to bear. From Mom's perspective, "Being an adoptive parent is a life as full as any I could ever imagine."

An Extraordinary Experience

"The result of divine directive" is how Mom describes the events that brought me into the fold of her amazing family. As a woman of deep and abiding faith, Mom had some special experiences as a foster and adoptive parent. Her firm and unwavering belief is that "It wasn't because of anything I had done that was wonderful or deserving of reward. It was grace. It was the will of One who knows the needs of each of His children."

It took place one early September morning in 1970 when Mom was 26 years old. She lived in southern Missouri back then, in a small three-bedroom house at the edge of town in a place called Mountain View. With three children under the age of five about to wake up, the sun not yet risen, she was standing at her bathroom sink, getting ready for the day. Mulling over the early morning "cobwebs" that get most of us started in the morning, actually thinking of nothing she can recall, she had an experience that set in motion a series of events that would eventually lead me to be her son. Words are inadequate to fully describe what occurred, but she was very much awake. Unexpectedly and without preamble, what happened seemed to play out like a dream. Mom believes that God is the same yesterday, today and forever; and He touches the lives of those who believe in Him in a variety of ways. She describes her experience the best way she knows how:

> *I was standing in front of the mirror getting dressed for the day and saw a baby boy with dark colored skin and black curly hair. I felt a voice speaking to my mind and was clearly impressed with words that referenced the boy before me. The voice said, "This will be your child, and his name will be called Lucas Daniel." The experience ended and I was left staring into the mirror. Having an experience like that would probably 'wig' some people out, or in the least be extremely unsettling. And NO ONE is a bigger scaredy cat than I am! But I took it all in and received it with a more curious feeling than anything else.*

This was Mom's immediate reaction; she tucked away the experience and pondered how such a thing could occur for one BIG reason. Mom is white! The baby in her experience, however, well... he was... black. But Mom believed and trusted in her experience. She remembers thinking, *"What does this mean? What should I do? How can I make this happen?"*

In an effort to be responsive to the impression left upon her, Mom went to the Howell County Missouri Division of Family Services to look into adopting a multicultural child. Mom looks back now in appreciation of an important life lesson; "Like the Lord needed my help! Division of Family Services didn't turn me down flat out," she recalls. "But I look back on my actions as an example of 'running before God.' God knew what He had planned. He had prepared me, and now all I really needed to do was wait for His timing."

Mom always encouraged us with a passage from the Old Testament in Proverbs 3:5-6. After hearing her rehearse, over the years, how I came to be her son, I can appreciate what the passage is trying to teach. *Trust in the Lord with all your heart and lean not to your own understanding. In all your ways acknowledge Him, and He shall direct your paths.*

This specific experience and all that was to follow wasn't in Mom's plan. Dorothy couldn't understand, but she trusted God and she believed the experience that she had while standing at her bathroom sink would come to pass. She believed this could be an opportunity to love someone who perhaps needed her at just the right time in his life. Recalling the example set by her fourth grade teacher Miss Chesnutt, that's exactly what she intended to do. With no clue as to when this child would come or how the experience would unfold, she decided to wait and let God show her what He was about to do.

Charlotte's Story

The real beginning of my story involves my birth mother, whom I haven't had contact with since before I was three years old. Out of respect for her, let's call her "Charlotte." In 1979 Charlotte was 19 years old and as a young person growing up had lived a pretty standard life. Lean in build, she stood about five feet, six inches with a prominent jaw line and sharp shoulders. Charlotte was an intelligent young woman and social workers made sure to inform Dorothy of this.

When Charlotte was 14, she began to run with the wrong crowd and was headed for a collision course with the consequences of life on the dark side of the streets. Charlotte began to drink in excess and became an alcoholic. She started to abuse her body with hard drugs, and eventually became addicted. Becoming addicted to drugs and having no job to support her habit, Charlotte used what was available and did the unthinkable, selling her body to get the money to feed the addiction that enslaved her – but just as often she traded sex for drugs.

Charlotte was placed in a mental institution for evaluation after an incident where she attacked a moving automobile with a butcher knife, wearing nothing but her birthday suit – "buck naked," as it was told to Mom by the caseworker. When she was in the mental institution the physicians discovered Charlotte was a few months pregnant. She could only guess that the father was a routine "John" or someone that provided drugs for a price.

Oddly enough, my birth mother's admittance to the mental institution was the first big blessing in my life. Mindful of her pregnancy, mental health professionals worked on stabilizing her with the right kind of medication, and she was off the streets. I was born on Saturday, May 19, 1979 at Truman Medical Center West Hospital in Kansas City, Missouri; premature and very frail. Charlotte's mind was severely affected by the drugs she had taken. She was so far gone, in fact, that when the doctors inquired as to what she would name her new baby boy, her choice was pretty peculiar, if not somewhat comical. She opted to call her first-born son Grandilow; the birth certificate was filled out and that was that. A caseworker with social services once told my foster mom that in situations like mine, mothers just named their kids anything. Inappropriate body parts and inanimate objects were just a few of the crazy names social workers had witnessed over the years. So I take solace in knowing that my first name could have been a lot worse!

After my birth there was growing concern for my future; less than normal birth weight and the possibility of impaired mental and physical functions were all scenarios that could affect my long-term health. The combination of a premature birth and other complications of the pregnancy caused considerable concern among the physicians appointed to my care. No immediate signs of autism could be found – which was a relief. Studies show that alcohol exposure during pregnancy is the number one cause of preventable mental impairment. There was no telling what problems would develop and surface over the ensuing years, assuming I received even the best care.

Jennifer James, in her book *Crack Kids: Cocaine's Living Legacy* (Do it Now Foundation 1998) writes, "The true extent of fetal exposure to crack is [hard] to guess. [T]he best estimate is that between 30,000 and 50,000 babies are born each year to mothers who use crack at some stage in their pregnancies."

Factor in the use of alcohol early in pregnancy and the likely prognosis for my future was grim. Christine Adamec and William Pierce, Ph.D. wrote about the effects of fetal alcohol. They said:

> *Although it is clear that consumption of alcohol during pregnancy is dangerous to the developing fetus, the negative effects are often confounded or even potentiated by other substances, such as tobacco as well as illegal drugs. In addition, after a child with FAS [fetal alcohol syndrome] is born, the environment she or he is brought up in before state or county social workers may become involved is often very negative to the child. Children with fetal alcohol syndrome are often premature and underweight with small heads and are likely to remain unusually small and thin. Many are mentally retarded. The average IQ of the FAS child is 68. They may also experience seizures and a host of other medical and psychological problems that are not outgrown as the child ages. Hyperactivity and a poor attention span are common problems. Other characteristics of FAS are growth deficiency and central nervous system*

*dysfunctions that lead to impulsivity, memory problems and
learning disorders.*

I can only imagine what the doctors thought as they considered the
case before them: a recovering alcoholic and addict who sold her body
for drugs had just become a mother to a boy she couldn't even properly
name. While I imagine no one voiced it publicly, the odds were stacked
against Charlotte and me. The doctors were determined to monitor
me and to give me as much care as they possibly could – not knowing
or having any control over the life that would be mine once I left the
hospital.

Over the course of the next ten days, the Division of Family Services
(DFS) in Kansas City, Missouri, sought to find a suitable surrogate to
care for me. DFS knew Charlotte did not have the mental capacity,
will, emotional maturity, or financial strength to give me the attention
I needed for normal development. In addition, drug involvement auto-
matically required alternative or foster care for a new child while the
mother was being assessed for the ability to provide adequate care in
the long term. At the time of my placement in foster care, the caseworker told Mom that when the nurse came to Charlotte's room at the
hospital and asked her if she would be able to attend the court hearing
for the baby's placement, Charlotte swung on the nurse and reportedly
broke the nurse's jaw.

Charlotte had family in Michigan, so the social workers spent
several weeks reaching out to her parents, siblings and other relatives
for assistance and possible surrogacy. No support came.

Imagine the casual observer who happened upon this scene; they
might have found it hopeless and logically conclude that the story ends
in despair; another tragic statistic and example of society's ills. They
could probably determine that if I survived, perhaps that would be the

real shame; because a life begun that way would surely only lead to a cycle of disaster. It would have been a perfectly legitimate question for someone to ask what kind of life it would be even if I were to live to be 10 or even 12 years old.

> *God's plans and His purposes are certainly more powerful than our life circumstances.*

Not only was the potential outcome for children exposed to fetal alcohol syndrome the grim picture painted above by Adamec and Pierce, the statistics also provided an unwelcome life sentence of neglect, a lack of love, potential incarceration, and living on the streets – a cycle waiting to ensnare me with drugs and addiction, just like Charlotte. Again, the casual observer could easily predict the outcome of this story would end in sadness, despair and quite possibly a destructive life-style. Unless, however, that observer believed in the grace and power of an almighty God and His son Jesus Christ; unless they believe that God's plans and His purposes are certainly more powerful than our life circumstances. Yes, unless the observer believed in a divine power they could readily conclude the prognosis to be grim indeed.

While, of course, I have no recollection of this time, I can imagine myself in an incubator in the neonatology ward of Truman Medical Hospital, struggling for life with every tortured breath from a heart and lungs still not fully developed. The effects of my mother's alcohol and drug abuse were lying dormant, ready to impact my life in the years to come. The concern of everyone involved was justified, as there was no plan and absolutely no hope. Yet, no one was aware of a broader, unseen reality, just waiting to be discovered.

This is just me musing, but I wonder if the same voice from heaven that spoke to Dorothy's heart nine years earlier spoke over this pitiful scene as well. Perhaps the Spirit of God said, *Wait, All is not lost. I will show you something.* Where some could easily conclude there was no answer, no plan, and life would soon be snuffed out; this scene of a severely premature baby fighting for existence against incredible odds is not the end of the story, but only the beginning of what God would do.

A little more than thirty years later I, a baby once named Grandilow, look back on how I came into this world and can plainly see that God was ever present from the beginning of my existence. He came to my aid in the womb, and saved my life. I don't know why I was the recipient of such grace, but I do know this: God preserved me in the midst of a difficult, unwanted and dangerous pregnancy. He has touched my life and I will forever be different as a result of His unmerited grace. I know it with every fiber of my being and will endeavor until the day I die to point men to God so that He can do the same thing for them.

Built for Something More

The experience and circumstances of my birth have taught me an invaluable life lesson about what it really means to feel valuable or have self worth. In a superficial society, as ours often tends to be, the current standard for self worth and personal value deprives so many people of the chance to realize their full potential. Whether it is looks, height, weight, intelligence or acquisition of wealth and fame, we are taught to glorify those who are the strongest, the most popular, the coolest, and the most "put together." We are taught to thumb our noses and beware of those deemed less than the norm, those who have a bad family, or those who come from the wrong side of the tracks. Sometimes we poke fun at the less fortunate because we don't understand a very simple and fundamental principle inherent in each life, that each of us is built for a greater purpose, for something more. We don't understand sometimes the value of every life so we trample on each other with irreverence and without regard for our own humanity.

In truth, I don't believe the aforementioned characteristics really matter. What really counts and what will make the difference for you in your search to fulfill your potential is to acknowledge (act on what you know) and embrace this fact: you are fearfully and wonderfully made. Regardless of your life circumstance and the "cards" you are dealt, each of us is unique and inherently special. And hey! It's OK to think you're special! A legitimately humble person knows what and who makes him or her special. They understand the gift and its source. If you can accept this fundamental truth, the seeds of success will take root and sprout an internal confidence that is authentic and ready to bear the fruit of lasting achievement. In order to be successful or to understand your worth you have to be complete on both the inside and out. Accepting yourself is the first step. You can't be complete unless you understand and fully appreciate the full measure of your value to yourself and others.

We must buy into the fact that we have inherent worth by the very virtue of our birth – solely because our heart beats and our lungs expand. During our formative years Mom was diligent in drilling this principle into each of her children's heads. It was a constant staple of our morning devotions. I'm not sure why devotions had to be at 5:30 in the morning, but as a kid it wasn't too much, apparently, to get up at the crack of dawn and sing songs before a daily lesson in my *Living in Covenant* workbook. A particular passage of scripture out of *Psalms 139* included verses I was instructed to read with frequent repetition. It's a passage I still visit from time to time to remind myself of God's incredible grace. The Psalmist writes in verses 1-3 and 13-14:

O Lord, you have searched me
  and you know me.
You know when I sit down and when I rise.
  you perceive my thoughts from afar.
You discern my going out and my lying down;
  you are familiar with all my ways.
For you created my inmost being;
  you knit me together in my mother's womb.
I praise you because I am fearfully and wonderfully made;
  your works are wonderful,
  I know that full well.
—NIV

I've come to believe everyone has a unique life story, one of purpose and one of destiny. But so often, tragically, many of us are either robbed of this realization or refuse to embrace it because of a variety of false barriers we've erected that limit how we feel and how we think. It's hard to believe you're valuable and deserve happiness when life's dealt you a blow and put you on the mat. I get that and I know it. Throughout various stages of my life I've struggled with the lingering effects of my birth mother's alcohol and drug abuse during pregnancy. However, I've been able to overcome that because of what I've decided about myself. Best-selling author Tony Robbins describes what I mean when he says, "It is not what happens to us that separates failures from success. It is how we perceive it and what we do about what 'happens' that makes the difference."

Verse 13 of *Psalms 139* speaks to the grace I believe is offered to every human being if they are willing to accept it. My birth mother made some unfortunate choices on her way to becoming addicted to alcohol and drugs. Anytime life throws a curve ball and things aren't going my way I remind myself that through all the choices Charlotte made, I was "covered in my mother's womb." Anytime I start complaining or wishing I was 6 feet 4 instead of 5 feet 7 (on a good day!), I remind myself of Who created me and for what purpose I was made.

No matter what your story, where you've been or what you are going through, accept this realization and let it take hold in your heart: you are fearfully and wonderfully made! According to a smattering of dictionaries, fearfully means, "with great reverence and heart-felt interest and respect." If the One who created us feels this way and respects us this much – then why sometimes don't we respect ourselves? To say it a different way, we are a work of art! We are better than any masterpiece Michelangelo could ever dream up! We are made with a tremendous and unfathomable amount of love and care.

Among the most rewarding responsibilities of my job with the Orlando Magic are the opportunities I receive from time to time to offer remarks to students and encourage them in their life endeavors. I've been fortunate to present to students of all ages, professional and civic associations, non-profits, teenagers in group homes, and even young adult prisoners in transitional housing.

I had one such opportunity on Thursday, September 24, 2009 when I kicked off a mentoring program for some students at *Cherokee School* in Orlando, Florida. A school built in the heart of downtown Orlando, it serves as a day school for kindergarten through sixth grade students who have had difficulty being successful in a regular school setting. I questioned the need for such a school and found the answer in their mission, "Changing Challenges into Opportunities." *Cherokee School* is the most restrictive educational placement for children with significant emotional and behavioral challenges that affect performance in the educational environment. Many of the students lack positive role models in their lives, and are often burdened with low self-esteem. Most of the students are from single parent households. Some have been victims of abuse, neglect or both and live in foster-care homes. Other students witness domestic violence on a daily basis. These childhood traumas affect their ability to learn and reach their full potential. As I prepared to share with them and read about the school's mission, my heart broke. I recalled the words from *Psalm 139* committed to memory through a steady drumbeat of recitation in our home growing up. These students' stories mirrored, in many ways, my own. I struggled as they do to overcome challenges not chosen, but thrust upon them. As I stood to speak to the 40 or so students, mentors and teachers gathered before me, I shared with them my story and how it ran parallel to and intertwined with theirs. With my closing remarks I told them that they were not built for failure. They were built for something more.

That morning before I left the office, I penned a few words that encapsulated what I felt. These were a few of the words I offered as encouragement to keep running, with a few words quoted from D. H. Groberg's poem, "Get Up and Win the Race."

> *You were built for something more*
>   *To desire, to drive on, and to dream*
>   *Built to set goals, and designed to achieve*
>
> *To overcome every obstacle is within your heart's core*
>   *Because you were built for something more*
>
> *You were not meant to fall in front of failure's face*
>   *You were built to live between mercy and grace*
>
> *To be unbroken, undaunted*
>   *Head and Heart Unbowed*

Built to be different from the others
    Your call is to rise above the crowd

Your gift is to win, to be a champion
    and above it all
To rise each time you stumble, to get up each time you fall

To begin tasks of leadership — Who will dream what can be?
    Who will realize each one of us is built to achieve?

So expect happiness and work harder than you've ever worked before
    Because from the very beginning of life
    You were built for something more

CHAPTER TWO

ADOPTED SON

*Somehow destiny comes into play. These children end up with
you and you end up with them. It's something quite magical.*
—Actress Nicole Kidman, Adoptive parent

My adoptive mother, Dorothy, has always instilled in me the value of faith, and the love and grace of God. The trajectory of my life could have been drastically different. I have adoptive brothers and sisters who also suffer from the effects of birth parents who abused drugs and alcohol. My favorite foster care brother, we'll call him James, suffered from a condition called *spina bifada* and was paralyzed from the waist down – likely because of the choices his mother made during her pregnancy. As a result, he passed away at the early age of 20. My sister Lesley suffers the effects of fetal alcohol syndrome because of choices her birth mother made as well. She is 36 as of this writing, but in many ways exhibits the mind of a three year old. But you know, she remains one of my favorite sisters, because of her inherent innocence. Lesley gives the best hugs at Christmas and is in a perpetual state of happiness, especially when she's eating Mom's turkey and pumpkin pie at Thanksgiving. The significance of being alive and whole is not lost on me. I don't take for granted this testimony that God saved me in a very real and tangible way. I am thankful for every breath and every heartbeat He allows me to have.

Special Delivery

The Division of Family Services (DFS) wasn't able to find suitable parents in my extended family to take care of me. So after ten days in the hospital, on Tuesday, May 29, 1979, I was sent to the foster care home of Dorothy Boyce – the same Dorothy who had had an experience nine years before about a dark-skinned baby boy coming to her home. She had completely forgotten about her experience, but, of course, God had not. When I arrived, Mom had five children either born or adopted between the ages of 5 and 14, plus various foster children aged 7 to 13. According to Mom, my arrival was accompanied by angels. I kind of laugh at that, but I'll let her explain.

School had just let out for the summer, so the children were outside kicking up their heels and playing like calves let out of the pen. Our backyard is one big slope, and much effort was called for as they played kickball on one of those bright and clear May days with redbuds budding, daffodils still abloom, and iris coming on. The streets and yards were littered with blossoms from the Bradford pear and dogwood trees; it was just a great day. I was watching the kids at play and enjoying the sight of their little legs churning up and down the hill, their arms flying about trying to get the ball, their laughs, cries of delight and groans of despair ringing through the air, when the phone rang. A brief explanation of the baby's medical condition and any special needs was the first line of business after I said that I'd be glad to help out and foster the baby.

Originally, I think the thought was that it would not be for long because they would be looking for family members who could provide protection for the baby. Well, later in the day this baby arrived. At the time, there were several girls age about 10-14, perfect ages for the arrival of a newborn baby! When the caseworker pulled up in the driveway I called to the children, "The baby's here!" and the girls came running from all corners of our yard. I was sitting out on a side porch, looking down on the sight, fascinated with what I was seeing: By the time the worker got out of the car the girls were gathered around the side where the baby was in his strapped car seat. As the worker waded through the small puddle of sweaty girls, "Excuse me. I'm sorry, honey. Can you move a little? Excuse me," I could hear their breath suck in, and then he finally got the strap unbuckled and the baby appeared, "Ohhhhhhh," in various tones and pitches, gushed out of the circled girls. I've always said that Lucas arrived at our house accompanied by a chorus of angel voices!

A New Name

The name chosen by my birth mother was pretty strange, yet that's what was on my birth certificate. The day I arrived at Dorothy's house she asked the caseworker if that's what they really had to call me. The response was, "Call him anything you want." At first the family thought of "Randy," because that would be a part of the name the birth mother had chosen, but then they noticed a striking resemblance between this little baby and some of my brother Bo's dearest friends, the twins, Jon and Jonathan, who "had fine little features, bright and happy personalities and were just so cute." Their last name was "Lucas" and so that's what the family decided to call me. My middle name came by consensus, according to Mom. "Lucas Daniel came to us as the whole name. Most of these decisions were made by the group method with a family vote. And though it sounds peculiar, even to me, it was about two more years before I remembered the day in 1970 when his little face and name were first presented to me."

One day in 1981, while standing in her bathroom, Mom had the same experience she had in 1970. She recalls seeing a dark skinned or black baby boy and felt the familiar words in her heart again. This time, the verb tense was different though. It was present. The words were, "This IS your child and his name IS Lucas Daniel." Mom was shocked. The normal hustle and bustle of life, of being a mom and a wife along with the continuous additions to her foster care nest had pushed the experience of 11 years prior completely out of her mind. Fortunately though, the expectation didn't escape her heart. Dorothy might have forgotten her experience, but the opportunities that evolved and the direction of her life proved a training ground of preparation pointing to the right time. Her quiet and unassuming preparation coincided with a need from the Department of Family Services at just the right moment. And she was ready to answer the call. What she had seen many years before had come to pass. It clicked. Grandilow was the dark skinned baby she had seen in her experience. As she thanked the Lord for such a neat testimony of His love, my mother began the application process and filled out the necessary paperwork with the court system to officially make me hers.

St. Patrick's Day 1982: Adoption Day

According to Mom, adoption day really began on May 30, 1979, the day I arrived as a ten-day-old baby. It would take almost three more years before becoming official, but I was welcomed as Dorothy's very own right from the start. As written previously, she was sitting in the family room of her home in Independence, Missouri watching the children play down in the "south 40" (our backyard). As Dorothy watched their little legs running up and down the hill as the children managed to play kickball on a terrain built for mountain goats and others of that ilk, she thought of how beautiful they were and how perfect their creation. She recalled the words of the Psalmist, "It is He who hath made us, and not we ourselves." The words confirmed to Mom that all of the children in her home, those present and those who might come, those who had been produced from her body and those who came from answering the telephone, those who had perfectly functioning beautiful bodies and those who through no fault of their own were somehow disabled, each came from the Lord. In an over-whelming blow she was made to feel the divine creation and perfection in *each of them,* not just the ones who were perfect to our human eyes. And in that moment, her role of steward was completely defined and she released "ownership" or any pride of involvement in the creation of any of their lives. In that moment of spiritual clarity, the children truly became His. A few minutes after this, the phone rang and a caseworker from social services asked Dorothy if she'd be willing to accept a tiny new baby affected by drug involvement (the implication being that he would need a lot of care and time as the drugs worked their way out of his system). Recalling the words of the Psalmist once again there was no doubt in Dorothy's mind that she would be lucky to provide a home for this needy child.

Time passed. Homes of relatives and homes of others who might provide a safe haven for me were explored, but never came to fruition. There were rare occasions when Charlotte, my birth mother, would be in a situation where she could accept a visit but those would be few and far between. As months turned into years the visits began to be met with fierce resistance by me. Mom recalls; "When Lucas reached about

17 months old he began to have a strong opinion about these 'outings' and it was definitely '*NOOOO!*' One day when I witnessed the sheer terror in this little kid as the caseworker came to the door, I realized that enough was enough." I have only one vivid memory of this early time in my life. I recall being placed in the car seat of a dark four-door sedan by a social worker and screaming at the top of my lungs for my mommy. Somehow, even at such an early age, I knew what seeing that social worker meant.

"Is it possible to remove this particular terror from this little boy?" Mom asked. "We might not be able to do everything, but was this something we should pursue?" Mom held some future hope that one day Charlotte would stop having the problems she had developed and would be able to provide a safe home for her son. As Mom grappled with the decision she wondered, "Is it necessary that Lucas sacrifice all developmental feelings of safety and security?" Following these difficult visits and her recollection of the unique experience in her bathroom nine years earlier, she took action. After talking briefly with the caseworker, Mom called a lawyer and proceeded with adoption. She was still going to be a steward, but now it was for life.

Before the adoption could be final, my birth mother had to approve. A part of me smiles at that. She clearly had a ton of her own struggles with drug addiction and alcohol abuse, but she had the presence of mind to want to meet the people who would be raising her son. I wonder if she thought it was her motherly duty to do so. In my heart that is a redeeming quality about her that I admire. Charlotte wanted to be sure that everything would be OK. When Dorothy went to meet Charlotte the caseworker told her that Charlotte was wearing every bit of clothing she owned: nightgown, jeans, sweatpants, shirt, sweater, a dress, it was all there. Mom assumed that perhaps Charlotte was homeless or at the least had nowhere safe to leave her clothes, so she wore them all. Whatever the reason, it makes her request to meet the people who would adopt me even more incredible, in my eyes.

I can only imagine what went through Charlotte's mind. Did she hesitate to approve the adoption because Dorothy was white? Did it even register? I wish I could understand what she was thinking and how she arrived at the decision to release me. I feel for her. And not knowing whether she is alive or dead, I pray for her. Not knowing whether I have other half brothers and sisters; and if so, I pray for them…whoever and wherever they might be. And while some could readily condemn my birth mother for the mess she made of her life, I have a different take on the situation. First, everyone makes mistakes. Without a full knowledge of the situation I refuse to judge her. I only hope that perhaps she's in a different place now and is stronger as a result. I will always be grateful that she chose to go through with the pregnancy, regardless of the risk her behavior caused. Charlotte easily could have had the unfortunate pregnancy taken care of and moved on with her life the way she wanted.

For Dot's part, it was one of the most stressful days of her life!

We met in a tiny little room at the Division of Family Services; seeing all of the cubicles for the caseworkers, I can tell you that I was quite grateful that at least we had walls and a door for our conversation! But, I was really nervous: "Oh please like me, oh please like me," became my mantra for the day! Out of respect for Charlotte and a sense of dignity for the occasion, I had worn my "Sunday best" – I think she very subtly "checked me out" – but I am so shy, and was so in awe of Charlotte and what she was willing to do for this child, I couldn't think of anything to say to her; I'm afraid I appeared a blob to her. It was the most important interview of my life, and I was no help.

Whatever she was looking for, however, perhaps she found, for she gave permission and signed the papers that day. I can only hope that she found this from me: an unspoken desire to help this lad grow to be a good man, as that was the true desire of my heart. I hope she found a fellow mother who honored her and what she had done for the world in allowing this child, as a tiny seed, to live. I doubt that she knew it, but I wished she knew that for all of the rest of my life she would be honored, not only by the child she had birthed, but by me as well — two people who would never have a Mother's Day without thinking of her with grateful hearts.

The easy decision for Charlotte would have been to abort; yet it wasn't the decision she made. While it is highly probable that she had no plan and couldn't take care of me, somehow, in some way she decided to keep me. Maybe...just maybe she too heard the voice that whispered, "Wait, I will show you something more."

When the court date was set – oddly enough on March 17, St. Patrick's Day – the most important order of business became the need for a new suit! Ah, J C Penney to the rescue! After rummaging through the racks, Mom found the PERFECT SUIT! The tiny little digs were plaid, to honor Mom's Irish ancestry, which combined perfectly with the colors of red, green, yellow, and stripes of black to honor my African ancestry. "It was a lovely little three-piece number, complete with its very own plaid clip-on bow tie!" recalls Mom. Along with the jacket and pants, the vest was solid red, trimmed along the front with plaid, and plaid pocket tabs on each side with a row of gold buttons. Gotta hand it to Mom. She knew how to dress her little ones! I'm not sure I'd pick a plaid suit today, but, what the heck! It was the eighties. I'm sure I was a sight to see. Mom's recollection?

Mercy, Lucas looked just gorgeous; there could not have been a prouder mom! And his brothers and sisters, each decked out in their Sunday best and getting a "pass" from school for the day, were bright eyed – all of them! Some of the children in our family at the time were foster children, but they, too, were all dressed in their finest dresses and suits. Pretty bows adorned the girls' hair, all wearing their special socks – the ones with the lace trim around the cuffs. Everyone was excited and none of us knew what to expect. It was a bright, sun-shiny day and since Kansas City has a great annual St. Patrick's Day parade, we agreed that if all went well in court, we would take our little army of children to the festivities after.

We filed into the waiting room of the Jackson County Juvenile Court in downtown Kansas City and attempted to wait silently in the orange and blue colored plastic chairs for our turn. That proved to be a challenge for a family of 12 at that time. Antici-pation dwindled to boredom for the children as the setting became familiar. You could tell who was there for adoption as the child's hair would be up in ribbons and EVERYONE looking spiffy! There were happy-shy smiles on everyone's faces. It was so cool. But the detention cases were not so cool – comings and goings through the door leading to the juvenile detention area; it was just sad to see kids who were trying so hard to look tough.

A little over an hour later our name was called. There we were gathered in a honest-to-goodness courtroom with wood paneling and official American and Missouri flags arrayed on either side of the bar. The tables and chairs were a brightly polished wood in the courtroom itself and the room was surrounded with a mahogany wainscoting about five feet high. It was very dignified and I could tell the children were so impressed. There was one long table for our family, a caseworker, and the guardian ad litem (which was the guardian assigned to Lucas to protect his rights). In my experiences with juvenile court the caseworker from the Division of Family Services usually sat at one end of the table, the guardian at the other end, and the family in the middle. We were a tight fit in that room.

Each of us quickly settled into the proper attitude that adoption requires. Big eyed and nervous we approached the bar of Judge Pendleton. Appearing very solemn, Judge Pendleton was large in stature, and ruggedly handsome. Sporting the customary bushy mustache of the time, he kept his questions serious and logical. Our case was professionally prepared and presented by a wonderful caseworker, Marie, and a lawyer who really knew his business and left no stone unturned. Of the question of race, I don't remember anything being said, but if race was important, I'm glad that Judge Pendleton happened to be a black man, for if the court had any question at all, I'm sure he would have addressed it.

Before long Judge Pendleton was banging his gavel, reading the official declaration of a successful adoption proceeding. He "ordered" us to go to the St. Patrick's Day parade, followed by a trip to Minsky's Pizza! Oh my goodness! I thought I'd never stop crying; it was such a significant moment and my tears reflected my gratitude to all who had made it possible.

Corralling 12 children to attend a parade was not especially easy among the crush of the crowd. Moreover it was the middle of March. While it was sunny, the cold wind picked up and before long so did our boredom with the floats. With the air getting cooler, our little band decided to head over to the Minsky's Pizza shop on Noland Road in Independence, where we all knew exactly what to do, and made a perfect end to a perfect day.

On St. Patrick's Day, 1982, my first and middle names were officially changed to Lucas Daniel. Mom went on to adopt four more children and St. Patrick's Day was known in our family as "National Adoption Day." Growing up, St. Patrick's Day was a "party day" to honor adoption in general and OUR adoption in particular, complete with pizza, cake, ice cream and pictures. Even now, Mom usually calls us and wishes us, "Happy Adoption Day" on March 17th, and she and my dad, without any of the children around, still have cake and a little celebration of their own, adoption having meant that much to them. She says that, for her, it will always be remembered as "the luckiest day of the year." It was such a lucky day, in fact, that when Mom married my step dad Larry they chose Adoption Day for their special day as well.

The Case for Adoption

Should race be a factor in adoptions? That is the question that *Time Magazine* journalist Jennine Lee-St. John addressed in an article released in May of 2008. The Multiethnic Placement Act (MEPA) of 1994 and the Removal of Barriers to Interethnic Adoption Provisions (IEP) of 1996 make it illegal to consider race when placing children with suitable families for adoption. But questions remain in our society as to the efficacy of trans-racial adoption. One thing I know is certain: There is a critical need to connect a large demographic of needy foster care children with loving families. Ms. St. John writes:

> *African American children who come into contact with the child welfare system are disproportionately represented in foster care, and are less likely than children of other racial and ethnic groups to move to permanency in a timely way. These children account for 15 percent of the U.S. child population but, in FY2006, they represented 32 percent of the 510,000 children in foster care. Black children, as well as Native American children, also have lower rates of adoption than those of other races and ethnicities (U.S. DHHS, 2008a; U.S. GAO, 2007).*

Hesitancy to endorse trans-racial adoption of children persists, in large measure, because of disagreement about the nature of adoption's goal. The goal, in my opinion, is to provide a stable, nurturing and empowered life to one who would otherwise be robbed of an essential birthright. Estimates of trans-racial adoption by the National Health Interview Survey show that only eight percent of all adoptions include parents and children of different races. Of the trans-racial adoptions that are occurring, only one percent involves a white woman adopting a black child. According to Kathy Shepherd Stolley, two percent of the trans-racial adoptions taking place involve women of other races adopting white children, while five percent of white women adopt children of other races.

Opponents of trans-racial adoption, white families with black children specifically, contend this practice undermines the goal of stability for needy children and can have consequences for the children as they develop. The stability argument, among others, is used *ad nauseum* as a reason for curbing this practice. Another reason is that white families cannot adequately teach a black child to deal with a white, racist society. This argument is flawed for a few reasons. Since when is it the gospel truth that we live in a white, racist society? And why are some so cynical and jaded about it? If it were true, does such a mindset help our society overcome that challenge? We'll discuss in depth the content of character in relationship to the color of our skin in chapter four. I will, however, offer this brief thought: our history of racism in this country must always be acknowledged but not at the expense of the brighter future we all seek. Our collective desire to be just, always working towards a more perfect union, holds true for the family unit as well. To actively advocate against trans-racial adoption based on the argument that we don't live in a color-blind society flies in the face of what our country is ultimately trying to accomplish. Racism in any form among any race is wrong and should be repelled with all the energy of soul, body, and mind. Regardless of skin color or background, parents should be teaching their children the virtue and benefits of diversity. We'll never achieve the inclusive society we seek if this isn't our practice.

The idea that black children raised by white families grow up to be "oreos" or betray their roots is another premise used among opponents. This is a name that was hurled at me frequently growing up, so I have some experience with it. I wasn't traumatized by it because my parents went to great lengths to instill a healthy self-image in me. I was comfortable in my own skin and didn't see myself as any different from the other black students in elementary school. That's just good parenting. They made fun of the way I talked, but I dealt with it. I could handle being teased because I was fortunate to have a proper perspective instilled in me regarding the bumps and bruises of life. Even as an adult working in government and corporate America the comment has often been,

"Lucas isn't really black." I couldn't tell you how black people should walk, talk, act or dress; but I can tell you what the corporate world expects. I can tell you what professional business attire and professional communication is. And parents, whether adoption is in the cards or not, should be instilling in children the skills necessary to be successful in a competitive world. If you cannot act, dress or present yourself professionally, I guarantee you won't be successful in business or in achieving your dreams. Some may argue white people have instituted this standard. That may be true as they are the majority. However, U.S. Census projections show that by the year 2050, that won't be the prevailing reality. Then, using the aforementioned argument will no longer be the case or a viable excuse for lower standards of expectation. A June 11, 2010 article in *USA Today* further confirms the evolving demographic. The article reported, "Nonwhite minorities accounted for 48.6 percent of the children born in the U.S. between July 2008 and July 2009, gaining ground from 46.8 percent two years earlier. The trajectory suggests that minority births will soon eclipse births of whites of European ancestry." I wonder what the argument will be then, because I'm willing to bet the standard for professionalism and success in the adult world won't change. For me, it isn't a black, white, Asian or Latino standard. It's a standard anchored to growth and maturity.

Another argument used by opponents of trans-racial adoption is that it is a plot by whites to steal black children, and that it is a form of genocide for blacks and other racial groups. This is laughable on its face and I would totally discount it — except there are people who actually believe this assertion. Thankfully, supporters of trans-racial adoption take a different view. They maintain through research that no science backs up the claims of opponents. Furthermore, there is consensus backed by studies that trans-racial adoption can serve in the best interests of the child. I know this to be true of my experience. According to authors Rita Simon, Howard Altstein and Marygold Melli, in their book *The Case for Trans-racial Adoption*, "Trans-racial adoptees do not lose their racial identities. They do not display negative or indifferent racial attitudes about themselves, and their families have as high a success rate as all other adoptees and their families."

Reports indicate that there are adoption agencies in some states that place greater emphasis on race when considering placement, but I don't ascribe mal intent towards opponents of trans-racial adoption. Much research has been done into this issue and regardless of what side of the debate you are on, the best welfare of foster care children of every race should be everybody's aim. In my experience, the impact on children themselves should be a determining factor. And given the situation I faced – having a mom and dad vs. waiting for one with my skin color – it is an easy call. I'll take a mom or dad, regardless of race, any day. I believe the ultimate goal of adoption will one day bring intelligent minds together on this issue.

The Evan B. Donaldson Adoption Institute sheds further light on this complex and sensitive issue. Research from the institute concludes a great deal of study on this topic over the last 35 years. According to the institute:

> *Research on this issue supports three key conclusions: 1. Trans-racial adoption in itself does not produce psychological or social maladjustment problems in children. 2. Trans-racially adopted children and their families face a range of challenges, and the manner in which parents handle them facilitates or hinders children's development. 3. Children in foster care come to adoption with many risk factors that pose challenges for healthy development. For these children, research points to*

the importance of adoptive placements with families who can
address their individual issues and maximize their opportunity
to develop to their fullest potential.

I can affirm all of those conclusions from my experience. I must note, however, some dissenting views from the Institute. The organization indicates the laws passed by congress to increase trans-racial adoption have fallen short and created "unintended consequences." According to the institute's report, "'Color-blind' adoption allows some white parents — who may not be mentally ready or have the appropriate social tools to parent black children — to raise youngsters, who may, in turn, experience social and psychological problems later in life."

I do not dispute their research, but I think the key word is "some." Yes, there are some misguided and not-so-adept parents out there; but this is true inside and outside of adoption. There is such a thing as a bad parent, just like there are bad doctors, lawyers, teachers and politicians. I hope that doesn't outweigh the many parents, lawyers etc. out there who are doing a stellar job. If we fall prey to this we've just affirmed the "one bad apple spoils the bunch" mentality.

I do agree, though, with a core finding of the Institute that parents, regardless of their race, should be exposed to education and training when considering adoption of a child who is of a different race. Beyond that, parents shouldn't be expressly or covertly prohibited from providing a home and stable life for a child of different skin color. Especially in light of the fact black children experience more hardship in getting adopted in the first place. Mom has adopted two trans-racial children and has fostered many more. She has a unique perspective having gone through this over 20 years ago when the environment and social norms were much, much different.

A friend of mine once expressed an interest in adopting a child of another race. She was white and asked about adopting a black child. My immediate response was the same one I feel now. I was excited she wanted to adopt a child and offer her home as an incredible gift to someone in need. The race wasn't even an afterthought. I wasn't able to produce an adequate response for her, as I have never adopted a "black" child. I've adopted a child that happened to be black but never a black child. Some would judge my approach as somewhat naïve and without regard to the needs of the child; that the child would need to have his/her heritage protected. Those are valid concerns, but in my mind and in my heart, raising a child to be a good person, to be a contributing member of society, to learn of his/her potential and take an interest in magnifying it to his/her greatest enjoyment from my perspective is the very nature of parenthood. It's the same for any race, any gender, or socio-economic circumstance. There is a lot that I just don't understand but I've worked and studied to provide what I could. I've never really had a feeling of "trans-racial" adoption, I just always felt like I would be very, very lucky if I could be the mom to someone who needed me.

I know I'm somewhat biased here, but my mom's feelings have literally been my experience. Irrespective of the race of a mom or dad is the fundamental fact that a young life is being joined to a family. Isn't that the point to begin with? We can figure out the best course of action for viable development. I won't dispute that. But hopefully we can agree that it can be done regardless of background or race.

There were three alternatives for me. One was life with a drug addict who had my skin color and background. At the time she was unfit for duty. She couldn't do it. The second was with an extended family member who shared my history and family tree. Social services looked for blood relatives to no avail. When reached, they declined to step up to the plate and even attempt to take a swing. The third option was with a white mother who had a wonderful home, and brothers and sisters who loved me. She stepped up to the plate, put her heart into it and swung for the fence.

After hearing my story, I'm pulled aside fairly often by individuals who are considering a trans-racial adoption. Their desire is to be the best parent possible and they question the effect their race will have on a foster child or the one they wish to adopt. Because the color of their skin and cultural background is different, they are fearful that somehow they will limit a black or Hispanic child and rob that child of the benefits of growing up amongst "their own."

My answer always echoes that of my mom. Love is the same in any language. There are some core values that every culture shares. Sure, there are nuances in language, food, communication, music, clothing, and faith. But there are also fundamental values that determine who we are and who we ought to be that run across cultures. Be a good parent, study the culture and expose your child to everything this "salad bowl" of a country has to offer. Instill in your child (foster, adoptive, or otherwise) the basics and then expose him to the mosaic of our culture. If you do a good job, in the final analysis, that child will grow up with an appreciation of not just his own culture but that of others as well. In a country that is increasingly inter-racial and multicultural it will be less and less of an issue as the winds of tolerance and inclusion blow from generation to generation.

Legacy of an Adopted Child

Once there were two women who never knew each other.
One you do not remember, the other you call Mother.

Two different lives shaped to make you one.
One became your guiding star, the other became your sun.

The first one gave you life, and the second taught you to live it.
The first gave you a need for love. The second was there to give it.

One gave you a nationality. The other gave you a name.
One gave you a talent. The other gave you aim.

One gave you emotions. The other calmed your fears.
One saw your first sweet smile. The other dried your tears.

One sought for you a home that she could not provide.
The other prayed for a child and her hope was not denied.

And now you ask me, through your tears,
the age-old question unanswered through the years.
Heredity or environment, which are you a product of?
Neither, my darling. Neither. Just two different kinds of Love.

—Author Unknown

CHAPTER THREE

A GIANT HEADACHE FOR THE TEACHER

Before success comes in any man's life, he's sure to meet with much temporary defeat and, perhaps some failures. When defeat overtakes a man, the easiest and the most logical thing to do is to quit. That's exactly what the majority of men do.
—Napoleon Hill

M om is and always will be an optimist. That's why she always likes referring to my first year of kindergarten as "an inexpensive pre-school." Two weeks in, it was firmly apparent to her that I would have to ride the merry-go-round of kindergarten one more time. The Problem Child, Dennis the Menace, or the Tasmanian Devil are a few adjectives that come to mind when trying to describe why. The consequences of a premature birth and being exposed to drugs and alcohol in the womb still lingered. I wasn't able to focus on my work and when I did concentrate, it didn't turn out that well.

Typically kindergarten is a social experiment in making friends, eating graham crackers and drinking chocolate milk, playing with Lincoln Logs and Legos and trying to color within the lines. Apparently, I had trouble with all five. Hyperactive and suffering from some learning disabilities, I gave my poor kindergarten teacher Ms. Waits a fit. After some tests it was determined that the learning disabilities weren't permanent cognitive problems and that I could do the work – I would just need to put in extra effort.

At one of my parent teacher conferences, late in the school year, my mother remembers Ms. Waits saying, "Well I went home last week with my usual splitting head ache – and I didn't immediately think of Lucas. I think he's doing better." And Mom, who really does love to laugh, had to sit there with a straight, "grown up" face and lots of pity for the dear teacher – bless her heart. I've never had an aptitude that lent itself to fast learning or intellectual heights. I recall throughout school that my classmates at times would barely study and do just fine while I struggled. Things just didn't come as easily to me as they did to others. They came – it just took a lot of studying and hard work to make sure that at the end of the day I knew my stuff.

Some Timely Advice from Mom

My friends went onto first grade while I stayed back for another year. It wasn't fun and I had enough sense to know that something was wrong. I felt like a failure. Wasn't that the definition of "flunking?" That's when Mom stepped in. She fed me a steady diet of optimism and encouragement. Her pep talk to me was this, "Lucas, don't buy into this failure nonsense because you aren't a failure. You can do anything you put your mind to. In other words, if I was willing to map out a plan of action and put my whole heart, mind, and strength into something, there wasn't any goal that was impossible to achieve. Mom began her

Star Wars Jedi-like mind experiment – with heavy doses of positive reinforcement. "You know, Lucas, you have a very high IQ; there's really nothing you can't do." I bought in.

> *There are no secrets to success. It is the result of preparation, hard work, and learning from failure.*
>
> **—Colin Powell**
> Former Secretary of State

When things wouldn't work out as I had hoped or I faced a particularly challenging obstacle in study, in music education, martial arts or sports, Mom would remind me of that simple phrase. Former Secretary of State Colin Powell described the principle this way, "There are no secrets to success. It is the result of preparation, hard work, and learning from failure." Mom was telling me not to be discouraged, to learn from the experience, to focus intently on my aim, to get up off the mat and not to quit.

The second principle Mom counseled me with was moral in nature. She has always been a strong believer that things happen in the heart, mind and spirit before they manifest themselves temporally. She said her second principle or key to success would serve as the foundation for anything I was to accomplish that was of lasting value. It isn't a monumental, earth-shattering principle. Simply put, she said, "Remember who you are and who you represent." Another way to put it would be to say, "BE GOOD!" Character and integrity matter and she was trying to tell me it was important to honor my Creator at all times and in all places. Mom was quick to instruct me that I was God's creation and I was saved by His grace. That meant I couldn't relax and hang my hat on that belief. The opposite was true. It was important, in light of

His grace, to live my life as an extension of His and do my best to point people to Him.

Mom taught me to turn my setbacks into stepping stones. I've never forgotten what Mom told me – that I could do anything I put my mind to and to remember who I am and who I represent. When I've kept her principles close to my heart even the bad times have been good. When I haven't, even the good times have been bad.

Show Em What You're Made Of

One thing that's always had an impact on me is how Mom and my teachers didn't give up on me. I was a terrible terror who wouldn't settle down and learn – perhaps a mask to hide that I couldn't. They could have easily dismissed my antics and failings as the result of the genetics I inherited. They could have concluded that with the obstacles and unfortunate circumstances surrounding my birth I would probably never amount to much. They could have just shuffled me through the school system and let the chips fall where they may. But they didn't. Instead they hunkered down and encouraged me to try again. I was always encouraged to "show the world what I was made of" and not to shrink from the obstacles and adversity that life inevitably would throw my way. Through every test and storm, even during the sunny days, Mom instilled in me her two principles for success. The instruction to focus, develop a definitive plan of action and then go for it won't always lead to a victory dance. But the other side of the coin – to remember who you are and whom you represent (integrity and character) will always allow you to feel good about every endeavor.

I'm OK with flunking kindergarten now and I don't shy away from the fact that I had to ride that merry-go-round twice. To do so would be to hide an invaluable life lesson, because if I hadn't gone through the process of disappointment and struggle, I wouldn't have been exposed to what it would take to accomplish the goals I set for myself. I've always had to work doubly hard to get where others arrive easily. I'm sure it's true for others as well, whether your pregnant mom abused drugs or not. And while I may have flunked my first year of school, through a lot of grace, hard work and love from family and educators the end wasn't quite like the beginning.

The day I graduated high school was a milestone that proved Mom wasn't just patronizing me and trying to make me feel good. I took her at her word and took consistent action toward my goal of academic achievement. High school graduation took place on a wonderful spring day in May 1998. The auditorium of Center Place Restoration School was packed with friends and family. The customary tears, songs and official pronouncements went by in a blur. One slot on the agenda was reserved especially for me and I waited for it in nervous anticipation. Principal Steve Ferguson finally called my name and I walked toward the podium, my heart pounding harder with each step. At my side was a black binder, which contained the valedictory speech I was about to give. As I stood at the lectern and began to speak, my voice cracked with a mixture of emotion and fear as the moment overtook me. It was an honor to graduate at the top of our small senior class, but more so because of how far I had to travel to get to that moment. As I closed one chapter of life and began to look towards another I offered my classmates and those in attendance these words from the Apostle Paul's letter to the Philippians, "Brethren, I count not myself to have apprehended: but this one thing I do, forgetting those things which are behind, and reaching forth unto those things which are before, I press toward the mark for the prize of the high calling of God in Christ Jesus.

CHAPTER FOUR

IDENTITY AND RACE

There is nothing wrong with America that cannot be cured by what is right with America.
—Former President Bill Clinton

The Color of Our Skin vs. the Content of Our Character

Growing up in a diverse home has given me a real appreciation for the unique offering each one of us has to give to the world. I have white brothers, white sisters, a black brother, and a sister who has special needs. Mom recounts a story from when I was about 13 months old and she was playing a common language game for toddlers with me. She would point to Mommy's eyes, Mommy's ears, Mommy's mouth, Mommy's hair, etc., saying the name of each and have me repeat it. She would stand in front of the mirror so I could see the differences as she then pointed out Lukey's nose, Lukey's lips, Lukey's ears, Lukey's hair, and Lukey's hands. We were playing one of the earliest vocabulary games played by mommies and their babies everywhere. As she tells the story she recalls me grabbing her hand at one point during her routine, and turning it over to look at it closely. I then held up my own hand next to hers and looked at it from every angle. "Yes, see. There's Mommy's hand and there's Lukey's hand!" Mom cooed. But I just turned them over and over, my face registering no enjoyment or fun at all, only seeing the seriousness of the situation. As my eyes began to well up with tears, my right hand came around and slapped my left hand – the clear message being "naughty hand!" "Bad! Bad!" I said while slapping my hand in apparent self-discipline. Hitting myself wouldn't change the situation, but what did I know. I was just a very little boy. Mom moved to correct my error immediately with the understanding that while the color of my skin was different from hers, we had much more in common than I realized.

I think it was that event and my mother's reaction to it and consistent instruction on valuing differences that has helped to crystallize my thinking on race and the many issues surrounding it. Mom taught us the principles Dr. Martin Luther King advocated long before I ever learned his name or read his famous speech in school. It wasn't just theory. It was real for us, and my brothers and sisters were encouraged from an early age to judge "by the content of one's character, not the color of one's skin." She took to heart his call and taught us that everyone was equal and good – just because.

Mom did an amazing job at creating an environment where color was never an issue among us brothers and sisters. So much so that when I came face to face with racism and prejudice later in life it shook me to my core and caused confusion; not between what's right and wrong, but with who I was as a person, my identity. For example, I was ten years old in the summer of 1989, when our new family went on vacation to Iowa. Mom had met a tall and handsome man by the name of Larry. He had three vibrant and quick-witted daughters, and while Larry's children were older and didn't move in with the rest of us kids, our new family was a reincarnation of the Brady Bunch. Larry was a man's man. I remain in awe of his many talents. It seemed he was an expert mechanic, able plumber, master carpenter/builder, chemistry teacher and man of God all rolled up into a singular lean frame that stood tall at about six feet one. Larry proved to be the missing piece to our family – making it strong and complete. An Iowa native and outdoorsman, Larry loved to travel so it was decided to go not just on a normal vacation, but an adventure. The trip was filled with firsts. It was our first vacation with our new step dad, Larry, our first time camping in the woods and sleeping in a tent, and the first time someone called me a nigger.

We pitter pattered along in Dad's vintage 1971 light blue and white Volkswagen van. The van was his pride and joy. The backseat converted into a bed, allowing us to ride in style down the highway while reading Hardy Boys books. Larry even custom made bench seats to make enough room for all of us to travel comfortably. He made more space with a simple construction of plywood and Styrofoam! Larry loved his reliable van, never mind the lack of air conditioning and heat! Let me tell ya, it was a real blast to ride in during the summer months of July and August. And you never fell asleep on the van ride home from school at night in December, January and February! I remember when the van crossed 100,000 miles on vacation one summer. I was silently praying it would break down so we could get a new car and be cool like the "Joneses." We all held our breath as the odometer turned. No such luck! I nagged both of my parents until Dad finally acquiesced and bought us a shiny new 1991 gray Plymouth Voyager. I called it a "mommy car" because it was a car like all of the other mothers drove. We couldn't figure out the air conditioning and on the way home from the car dealership my sisters Tara, Lesley and I all froze in new-car excitement!

But back to our adventure vacation. We rode a ferry across the Mississippi River, watched the lock and dam on the river at Keokuk, Iowa, ran through the cornfields at the "Field of Dreams" movie set in Dyersville, Iowa, and visited Grandma Boyce, Larry's mom, at the nursing home in Mason City, Iowa. Over 90 years old at the time, Grandma Boyce was new to our lives and we were excited to meet her. For this trip our family was down to three children, the two girls and me. The girls wore dresses and ribbons to meet Grandma Boyce and I wore my nice clothes as well. The five of us filed out of the beat-up Volkswagen and proceeded inside. It was a sunny day in Iowa and as we walked up the sidewalk to enter the nursing home where Grandma Boyce lived, wheelchairs were lined up on either side of the wide entry with residents sitting in them enjoying the warmth of the day. But as we made our way through the hallways of the nursing home my joy and excitement turned to confusion. I vividly remember a group of elderly ladies sitting casually in the hallway as we passed by. All of the sudden one looked up at me, pointed and got the others attention, "Hey look at the little nigger boy!" I guess they were as shocked to see me as I was to hear that derogatory word directed my way.

I wasn't prepared for the racial curve ball and it momentarily shook my confidence. And, moreover, it stung. *How could someone yell names at another human being like that?* I wondered. They didn't know me and had never met me. Yet they were quick to call me names and make a snap judgment based solely on the color of my skin. I assumed, mistakenly, that everyone was raised to be color blind and tolerant; or at least was taught, "If you don't have something nice to say, don't say anything at all." The ladies were taught a set of principles or rules that were a relic of another generation, a darker time.

Whenever anything like this occurred, Mom seized the opportunity to embrace a different perspective, one that would always restore my confidence. She was quick to point where true identity, confidence, and sense of purpose reside... with God. She was equally quick to instruct me that because I was created by Him and saved by His hand, my response to these tough situations had to be one of "turning the other cheek." She counseled me to live my life as an extension of His and do my best to point people to God in all I said and did, no matter what they might do or say. It was a tough pill to swallow, especially when a racial epithet is hurled your way. Regardless of the situation, the quiet, steady counsel remained the same. I haven't always lived up to this counsel and would be remiss if I pretended otherwise. I deeply regret the times when I could have responded in love instead of anger or fear. There are times when I haven't been a witness for what I know is right and just.

I'm thankful for the counsel Mom gave me, because it got me through a few tough situations associated with my race growing up. I readily acknowledge that most children (of any race) deal with issues and challenges beyond their control throughout childhood, and do not pretend my experiences to be something extraordinary. What I do offer, though, is a different perspective on the personal impact of challenging situations. Primarily because our home was so diverse and the circumstances we faced were uniquely complex.

Teased for Having a White Mom

One such circumstance occurred while in school. The other black kids at our elementary school, Thomas Hart Benton, teased me incessantly. It was perplexing because they were black. I was black. Whatever could the problem be? The problem wasn't me, *per se*, but my white mother and our big diverse family. As I rode the bus to school they would go on and on about how my mother was a whore and had a bunch of kids from different fathers. Even in hindsight I don't understand why they ganged up on me. We all lived in the same economically depressed, lower class neighborhood. Shouldn't we have banded together? Surely there were bigger fish to fry; but, then again, they were misinformed kids who I'm sure know better now.

The black kids in our neighborhood never let me into their clique. The logic was because I had a white mom and white brothers and sisters, I wasn't one of them. I couldn't understand it and it hurt. I was black like them and lived a stone's throw from Hocker Heights, the government housing projects they grew up in. Somehow, even though I was poor like them, and black like them, I wasn't good enough to be accepted by them. They called me a lot of "nicknames," but the nickname that has stuck with me was "Darky." The translation is that my skin was too dark and my mother was too white. It was a no-win situation. To them, I was different. They would give me the business over and over on the bus to and from school, but in the back of my head was the counsel my mother gave me; *You know where your identity resides* [with God] *and He requires a better response.* She also quoted Romans 8:28, which says, "All things work together for good for those who love God and are all called according to His purpose." So I let the insults and the name calling fuel and teach me. On the one hand, it taught me never to treat someone as less than me, regardless of who he is and what I think of him. On the other hand, the experiences fueled me with an even stronger desire to succeed – to prove them wrong – that I wasn't less than them and I deserved to belong.

A Bad Night in Buckner, Missouri

Another incident took place on a Friday night in seventh grade. I was spending the night with a friend from school, Chad Vermeland. Chad lived in Buckner, Missouri, a little rural town about 20 minutes east of Independence on 24 Highway. We were walking along the road to a convenience store to buy some snacks when a red truck with oversized tires and a Confederate flag imprinted on the back window drove past. As the truck drove by a white man stuck his head out and yelled, "You better get your nigger ass out of town." I assumed he was addressing me because my friend Chad was white. He then peeled out and turned around in pursuit. Chad and I took off running and cut through a field to escape. I'm thankful he didn't cut through the field and take the same short cut to safety we did. He certainly could have with his 4x4 truck. Needless to say we didn't venture out to purchase the snacks. I, for one, was too afraid to leave the house and shudder to think what might have occurred if he had caught up to us.

Difficulty Dating

While in school, I encountered another obstacle due to my race. I attended a school where I was one of a few black students enrolled. Generally this didn't present a problem or involve major issues. I had a wonderful time in high school and made many friends of different races both on campus and elsewhere. My race became an issue when I reached the age that I realized girls no longer had cooties and I wanted to date. Interracial dating, in some places in our country, still carries certain stigmas and is frowned upon. Whether it's tradition, prejudice, or general discomfort, the reasons for this are many. In my experience most of the girls, – black, white, or other – that I was interested in never expressed any hesitancy because of my race or biracial upbringing. Setbacks came when their parents found out. I didn't always get the best treatment or the welcome mat. I certainly wasn't the guy who had ulterior motives and was a little too smooth for their comfort. I was the guy unable to string a sentence together to ask a girl out most of the time. So when I did muster the courage to "swing for the fence" and connect with a girl, it was puzzling to get resistance without cause.

I didn't understand that the resistance existed likely because they didn't want their daughter dating a black guy. I was a pretty good teenager who made good grades, played on the basketball team, and was involved in ministry at church. While I fully admit I was an immature teenager and a general curmudgeon at times, I didn't think I was that bad!

Stereotypes are another reason I believe I ran into trouble. I know in my heart these were good parents who loved their daughters deeply and I always wondered if perhaps social pressure, or "what others might think" was the cause of their reticence to embrace me as the "boyfriend."

There was an instance where I was dating an amazing girl only to find out that she was withholding from her family the true nature of our relationship. It stung. I had no idea of her discomfort and was oblivious to her dilemma due to an upbringing that taught me to look more at similarities than differences. To her family, I was "just a friend."

The experience caused an internal struggle for me. We held hands but hadn't kissed. I couldn't bring myself to pull the trigger. I never wanted her to have to lie about who her first kiss was with to family and friends. It really hurt and I wondered what there was to be ashamed of. I tried to be a model student maintaining good grades. I was president of the student council, and involved in church ministry and high school athletics. Why wouldn't a parent want me to date their daughter? It got so bad that when I did date a girl whose family was OK with it, the parents would go out of their way to tell me they were happy I was dating their daughter.

Rejected By Family

When it came time for making a commitment to live for Jesus Christ, Mom asked my uncle, a minister at our local church, to perform the baptism. As an adult he'd been taught by deeply misguided individuals that African Americans were a lesser species and the result of bestiality with monkeys or apes; therefore rendering the race unfit for the body of Christ. He told my mother, his sister, that he could not go forward and baptize me because of what he believed. Saddened by the situation, Mom instead chose a close family friend, Jack Hagensen, who gladly accepted and helped me begin my path with Christ.

Mom tells of that experience:

As I look back, I first realized how blessed I was because I had to make a ten hour road trip with my brother not too long before Lucas' baptism. As we drove along he told me about these beliefs that had been put before him and what he thought of them. I didn't make a judgment towards him because I thought that this was a path he was traveling and he didn't need me to correct him; God would do that in His time. But I knew from my brother's own lips what he believed at that time. At the same time, this same brother was teaching Lucas in his Sunday School class. I can't tell you how often my brother would come and tell me what a good student Lucas was, how he was so attentive and how he asked such good questions, showing that he was interested and curious about the scriptures and God. This confirmed for me that my brother knew of the sincerity of Lucas' heart and when Lucas asked for baptism, I didn't hesitate to ask my brother to do this for him. He said yes, and we proceeded, but at 10 p.m. the night before the baptism was to occur, my brother came to my house and, sitting on my couch, told me that he couldn't do it. I sat there on a little stool in front of my brother and prayed a silent prayer that somehow I would not be alone, that I would know what to do to protect my son from rejection and, at the same time, not cause my brother sadness. And at that moment, from nowhere seen with a human eye, an arm came around my shoulders and hugged me, comforted me, strengthened and supported me. I knew I wasn't alone and that I could find a solution to this dilemma. Thankfully, several months before this time, Jack Hagensen had suddenly stopped Lucas and me in the parking lot at church to tell us that the Lord had work for Lucas to do if he would remain faithful. Now my mind immediately went to that experience and I knew that Jack would baptize Lucas. Late as it was, I called him immediately and he agreed without needing an explanation. As the months and years went by my brother remained very interested in Lucas and his life, and before his death in 2009, he knew that he loved Lucas.

Some have asked if these incidents upset me or affected me in a negative way. Thankfully, I've been able to grow from each one rather than be corroded or jaded from the negative experience. I view racism and prejudice as another form of ignorance. In most cases people act as a result of their upbringing, education or even a negative experience they themselves might have had. It's troubling that someone would have a preconceived notion about another individual because of skin color, background or language. It would be even more troubling if there wasn't information readily available to enlighten the minds of anyone willing to open their heart to another way of thinking.

The negative encounters I've had because of race serve as a catalyst for me to try to build a bridge of understanding from one culture and race to the other. The obstacles and unfortunate incidents didn't sap me of hope, but instead helped me grow, develop fortitude and cultural sensitivity. The racial awakenings have focused my efforts on being friendly to anyone and everyone irrespective of their race and background. I'm more conscious and accepting of the diversity inherent in each human being. Through it all I've learned that differences aren't something to be afraid of and attack. On the contrary, diversity should be something we each seek to understand and then embrace.

I'm not one to wish the unfortunate experiences associated with my race never occurred. I do wish my uncle had baptized me, though. Thankfully, I've never had to deal with the burden of bitterness and resentment. As I grew I came to understand that it was pure ignorance that led him to make that decision, which paved the way for an incredible lesson. In my twenties my uncle and I became strong friends. He matured and came to realize that his previous beliefs about black people were off base, deeply bigoted and profoundly mistaken. When I moved to Washington, D.C., my uncle would send me letters of encouragement and inspiration from time to time. We kept a close correspondence through mail and I have deep affection for him to this day. He heard me share at a large church gathering a few years back. There were almost a thousand people in attendance, but it meant more to me to have him there to support me than the hundreds of others gathered for the worship service. He had suffered

> *If we are willing to seek the common ground that comes from seeking higher ground, a post-racial society is nearer than we think.*

a severe stroke and was unable to speak properly. I met him and Mom after the speech and he gave me a big hug. The hug conveyed more than "Atta boy, good sermon." In that moment a bridge was crossed. Through a simple embrace he sent me a clear message: *I'm sorry, I know better now. I love you and I'm proud of you.* All prejudice melted away and the impact on me will last as long as I live. Because of that one instance of reconciliation, I believe it will always be possible to bridge the gap between races. If we are willing to seek the common ground that comes from seeking higher ground, a post-racial society is nearer than we think.

I wouldn't change the incidents and issues caused by my diverse upbringing and race, even if I could. Each unfortunate experience taught me profound lessons of perseverance, patience and forgiveness. Because of racial struggles I've encountered and the impact on my development, I believe that "Everything happens for a reason." If utilized in the right way, everything that happens to us (good or bad) can ultimately be a tool in our hands to help us get to where we want to go. We don't know what the road ahead may bring. Sometimes it will be good, but in every life "stuff" or adversity happens. Adversity has happened in my life. I've recounted some of the occasions where the adversity was related to race. More often than not, the tough times have been a result, not of skin color, but of the beating of my heart. Everyone will get rocks thrown at them throughout life. The lesson I hope to instill is this: when adversity happens you don't have to be a victim. You can take the tough times and transform them into an opportunity to empower, to build a bridge, and propel yourself toward achieving your goals. Remember, "All things work together for good to them that love the Lord and are called according to his purposes."

If You Can Look Up You Can Get Up

Race still matters in America, but it shouldn't deter us from continuing our forward march towards equality. Former President Bill Clinton said, "There is nothing wrong with America that cannot be cured by what is right with America." I'm a glass half full type of guy. My view has always been that there are more positive things taking place than negative in the world. So why not use the positive to overwhelm the negative? It will always be important for us to continue our national conversation on race and its impact on who we are and how we interact with each other.

My friend Alphonso Jackson, former secretary of Housing and Urban Development (HUD), once gave me some important advice. He is one of many who came of age during the civil rights movement. Fighting for equal treatment and marching on behalf of civil rights during the 1960s was a dangerous and courageous cause. Recorded for history and etched for all time are the acts of violence perpetrated on those who stood up on behalf of civil rights. Their antagonists were cowards who utilized fear, intimidation, fire hoses and attack dogs to do their bidding. Once in his office at HUD, Secretary Jackson rolled up his suit pants and showed me some scars on his legs, teeth marks left over from the cruel bite of dogs. For him, the scars he bears serve as a permanent reminder of adversity, but also triumph. He told me something I will never forget. Secretary Jackson said, "Lucas, if you can look up you can get up."

> *If you can look up you can get up.*
>
> **—Alphonso Jackson**
> Former Secretary of Housing and Urban Development

His words are powerful and can serve as encouragement for us as individuals and as a nation. We've been knocked down by bigotry, injustice, ignorance, misunderstanding, and hatred. It's time that we get up. In many ways the election of our first bi-racial President, Barack Obama, represents an awakening from our national slumber. We are just beginning to get off the mat and it's encouraging to see. We have a lot of individuals and forbearers to thank for what we have and where we are today. In my generation I can look to former Secretary of State Condoleezza Rice, General Collin Powell, former Congressman J.C. Watts, the Reverend Jesse Jackson, and Congressman John Lewis. Then there are trailblazers of the civil rights movement like Dr. Dorothy Height, Dr. Martin Luther King Jr., and Robert F. Kennedy. The list goes on and on of both white and black leaders who came together to achieve what we have today.

We should be especially mindful, though, of those individuals, from every race, who believed enough in what was right to sacrifice and put their lives on the line. They will never be called congressman, civil rights leader, or president. Yet their contributions to where we are now were vital to our progress. Men and women of courage, they were slaves, and in some cases slave masters whose conscience overwhelmed them. Regardless of who they were, our forbearers serve as the silent heroes of history. Their reach and influence go back decades, generations, and even centuries. And while we may not know their names or recognize their faces, we honor their sacrifice.

Before diversity, inclusion, and a post-racial society were ever buzz words and principles our country aspired to, civil rights leaders, known and unknown, made our appreciation and advocacy of these aspirations possible. A few harsh experiences have taught me to be grateful for their heroic efforts. Dr. King suffered far worse than receiving a racial slur or having difficulty dating. My experience has driven home the imperative to seek common ground and embrace tolerance and inclusion. Ultimately embracing diversity hinges on understanding and appreciation for the unique nature each individual has to offer. Diversity and inclusion is not just a politically correct utopia. It is a call to action from those who have paved the way before us. It remains our responsibility to advance it from generation to generation until Dr. King's dream is fully realized.

We all come from different backgrounds, upbringings and frames of reference, yet we share a common bond in our desire to participate in the American dream of boundless opportunity. As we seek to bridge the gap, the responsibility for each one is to do our part – and by our example, by our individual and collective passion, assist in the work of our nation to become more inclusive and more welcoming to all. This should be our goal and our commitment. No matter our ethnicity, gender, background, generation of birth, level of education, or religion, we should never settle for less than who we were meant to be. In a rapidly changing and increasingly color-blind society, we have an opportunity to prove to the world that our diversity is ultimately a unifying force; and that our varying backgrounds will be what continue to make this nation a beacon of hope and opportunity for the entire world. To quote Dr. King, "We cannot walk alone. And as we walk, we must make the pledge that we shall always march ahead. We cannot turn back."

CHAPTER FIVE

THREE DREAMS

*We must be willing to let go of the life we have planned,
so as to have the life that is waiting for us.*
—Joseph Campbell, American Philosopher

Nothing happens unless first a dream.
—Three Time Pulitzer Prize Winner Carl Sandburg

Christmas Rituals

Growing up, there were a few rituals my brothers and sisters came to expect with the onset of Christmas. The day after Thanksgiving we would open up the old wooden trunk that served as our family coffee table and footrest 11 months out of the year. No more than two feet wide and about three feet long, it contained the Christmas lights, a few homemade and some store-bought ornaments. It also housed personalized stockings of different colors and designs custom-made for each child. Mom crafted each one according to our various interests, hobbies and goals. For instance, I played the piano and wanted to be a doctor when I was younger. So Mom set out and found a small hand crafted piano and doctor figurine to sew on my red, green and white checkered stocking. She was an able seamstress, which came in handy in other ways as well. Because the family didn't have much money and we were a pretty full house, the majority of the younger children's clothing was created from Mom's trusty pale green Singer sewing machine. When I was six-years-old, Mom used her gift as a seamstress to enhance my education experience. We were learning different colors and applying them in our studies. I still recall the Thursday night one winter when Mom worked until the wee hours of the morning to finish making a purple jump suit. She finished in the nick of time. Hot off the press I proudly strutted my stuff at school that Friday. Not so sure I'd rock a purple jump suit today. Mom made the fashion decisions back then.

Blessed to get by, we didn't let economic constraints prevent us from celebrating the holiday season. We always managed, with the power of our imagination, arts and crafts, and a little elbow grease to make the house and especially the Christmas tree look spectacular. The lights were a patchwork of different colors and combinations. Our simple garland was complimented with strings made of popcorn and dried cranberries. Armed with an assortment of multicolored construction paper, Elmer's Glue, string, silver and gold glitter, scissors and a box of crayons, we went to work just after Thanksgiving to make the tree look perfect. Homemade ornaments, some with our latest official photo from school attached and other decorative flare, all dotted the tree. I didn't fully grasp how poor we were, but the love we shared was clear to see.

Mom allowed us to open one gift, of her choosing, on Christmas Eve. This was, more often than not, a pair of socks and some new pajamas she had made. As kids we could always count on there being more fruit than candy in our stockings and warm cinnamon rolls for breakfast in the shape of a Christmas tree. There was one practice in particular that became a highlight of our day and a moment we all looked forward to. Mom and Dad would lead us in a brief period of worship before opening gifts. Our reflection was more than the customary reading of Luke, chapter two. As ten of us, and later six then four gathered at the foot of our simple evergreen, Mom would break open a book and read to us a story entitled *Better Than All Your Planning.*

As the story goes, a long time ago in a forest atop a hillside there was a mother tree and her three little trees. The mother tree asked the others what they wanted to be when they grew up. The first tree responded that he wanted to be a baby's cradle. "I think a baby is the sweetest thing I have ever seen," it said. The second tree boasted that he wanted to be "something important, a great ship, strong and stately to carry cargoes of gold across many waters." The last tree was quiet at first, not wanting to reveal its dream of the future. At last, with much prodding, the tree spoke. The little tree's one wish was to grow ever taller – so tall that when men and women would see it they would look to heaven and think of the Creator. "I don't want anything but to stand here and point men to God," the third tree exclaimed.

The story goes on to tell how in each instance the trees did not accomplish their original design. In fact, as the story unfolds each tree is at one point despondent, heartbroken and discouraged when things do not turn out as it had dreamed. In each instance, at the tree's darkest moment, a voice would whisper, "Wait, I will show you something." The first tree was torn apart, but crafted into a makeshift manger for cattle to eat from. The meaning of the tree's existence changed when a mother named Mary used the manger as a cradle for her newborn child. The tree ended up being a cradle after all. "In all my dreams I never thought to hold a baby like this!" cried the little tree. "This is better than all my planning. I'm part of a miracle."

Neither did the second tree, which wanted to be a large ship, fare so well at first. It became a small fishing boat owned by a simple Galilean fisherman named Peter. The tree lamented its lot in life. "To think my life has come to this! Just an old smelly fishing boat, and Peter not a very good fisherman, either." This tree, too, heard a voice that said, "Wait, I will show you something more." It turned out this little boat would hold precious cargo, after all, and be part of a miracle. One day Jesus came and sat down in the boat, taught the people by the shore and told Peter to launch his nets out into the sea. The boat trembled underneath the weight of wonder at his fortune and the unexpected turn of events. "In all my dreams, I never thought to carry a cargo like this! I'm part of a miracle. This is better than all my planning."

And the third tree, the one that just wanted to stay on the hillside and point men to God, was torn apart and made into a rough cross. The tree was devastated. "Why couldn't they just leave me alone!" it cried. Not knowing whom they would kill on it, the tree cried out in despair. This was definitely not in his plan. But then the tree heard a voice that said, "Wait, I will show you something." That tree became the cross upon which Christ gave His life for the world. As the miracle took place the tree began to understand. "This is wonderful," he thought. "I'm part of a miracle. In all my dreams I never thought to point men to God in this way. This is better than all my planning."

The final result for each of the trees turned out to be better than anything they could ever dream or imagine. It was better than all of their planning. Their despair, heartache and disappointment were turned to joy when they realized the larger purpose for their creation. They were built for something more.

Each Christmas morning growing up, this is the story that we would hear. Its purpose was three-fold: the first was to offer us a different perspective for any disappointment or feelings of failure we might have harbored. The second was to teach us to dream. The third was point us to God and remind us that our dreams are only fully realized in Him. The yearly ritual of hearing this story reminded my brothers, sisters and me that we were part of a larger design, and our lives were full of purpose. And it holds true for all of us. We are built for something more. Most importantly, to point men to God in all that we do, wherever we are. As I've grown up and spent more and more time away from home during the holidays, I've had my own personal devotion on Christmas morning and it begins the same way as it did when I was 12: with a reading from the Book of Luke and the story of the *Three Trees*.

This story has come to mean even more as I have set out to try and accomplish my dreams. Its lesson has made a lasting mark on my life. The significance has stayed with me through the years: from a little wide-eyed boy on Christmas morning into my early twenties at the University of Central Missouri to serving at the White House in various capacities, and now as an executive with the NBA's Orlando Magic. The lesson for me and I hope, you, hits home. We can plot and plan, and pursue our dreams. Sometimes things won't turn out exactly as we hope. Sometimes we have to regroup, re-plan, and re-direct. Sometimes it means going in an entirely different direction altogether.

One thing is certain though; when I've applied Mom's two keys to success: 1. That we can do anything we put our minds to, and; 2. always remember who we are and who we represent, no matter what the original design, the end result has been something more wonderful than I could have ever conjured up to begin with. Because of what I have seen over the past few years I'm a strong believer in this next statement. When I've pursued both my goals and God's glory, the experience has been better than all of my planning. If you will pursue your dreams while giving of yourself to worthy causes that build and uplift those around you, you will find that the two will become one, and your determinations will become your destiny. As I have said before, when hard work and determination meet grace and opportunity, anything can happen.

When I was about 12 years old, I began to look towards the future and dream. In a sense I went through the same process as the three trees. The questions began to form in my mind: *What does the future hold? What do you want to accomplish? Who do you want to be?* Mom always encouraged her children to dream. So that's what I did. I came up with a series of goals, wishes and desires. I went to work planning how to make each one a reality. When high school graduation arrived, three principal dreams rose above the others in importance. I had no idea at the time how to make them come true. And while events didn't unfold precisely as I planned, the end result was better than all of my planning.

Michael Jordan vs. Magic Johnson

The 1991 NBA finals match-up between the Bulls and the Los Angeles Lakers was billed as a confrontation between two of the game's most charismatic figures, Michael Jordan and Magic Johnson. If you're even a moderate basketball enthusiast, you probably remember the moment all too well. If you're an avid fan you remember where you were and where you watched the game. I was in fifth grade in our family room when I saw it. It was game two at Chicago Stadium. The Bulls lost game one and their home court advantage for the best of seven series on a last second shot by Sam Perkins by a score of 93 – 91 the Sunday before. Game two on Wednesday June 5, 1991 would test the resolve of an underdog team that local media said didn't have "what it took" to defeat the veteran Los Angeles Lakers.

At the time, I was oblivious to the drama and none of us could conceive of the eventual dynasty that would emerge over the next decade. Not really knowing any of the back story of the Chicago Bull's titanic struggle to reach the pinnacle of NBA basketball, and for the most part unaware of professional basketball in general, I found myself channel surfing that night and stumbled upon one of the greatest moments in professional sports. As I was cruising through the channels, with the attention span of someone who had overdosed on a lot of sugar, I came across NBC. I found myself setting the remote down and focusing intently on the basketball game unfolding before me. I had never watched an NBA game before and the broadcast announcer kept talking about these two players Michael Jordan and Magic Johnson.

Being in the fifth grade, I had just begun to take an interest in the sport that year. For me, playing basketball was an awkward, comical sight to see. For one, I was in the midst of a pubescent growth spurt (which would prove to be short lived!) I was an awkward, lanky kid just struggling to grow into myself. My glasses (more commonly known as magnifying glasses) were brown coke bottle knock offs. They took up most of my face giving me that unmistakable appearance of a Steve Urkel look-alike. To top it off, for some reason I insisted on wearing a preppy looking polo shirt under my regular uniform. Talk about lame! With white socks reaching up to my knees and old school black and white British Knights for sneakers, I thought I was the coolest thing on earth. Good thing it was only the fifth grade.

As I watched the middle of the third quarter unfold the spectacle drew me in. Michael Jordan hit 13 shots in a row. *Who is this guy?* I thought. *He's incredible!* Later I came to identify with his story and take his life lessons to heart. He became an example of what is possible if you're willing to work harder than anybody else. MJ was a guy who had faced failure and "temporary defeat." Cut from his high school basketball team, he overcame challenges, rejection and obstacles to become, in my opinion, the greatest player the game has ever seen. I looked up to him because of his talent, but more so because of his determination and drive to succeed. I had missed most of the game but tuned in on time to witness that unbelievable lay-up in the fourth quarter. It is that moment that still sticks out in my mind 19 years later.

With seven minutes and 44 seconds to go in the fourth, Jordan received a pass at the top of the key. MJ went up for a dunk when a defender blocked his path. He then switched his dunk into a left-handed hook shot in midair. The acrobatic act earned him an ESPY for move of the decade. The Bulls went on to rout the Lakers 107-86 as Jordan scored 33 points on 15-18 field goal shooting. They would go on to win the next three games in Los Angeles and their first of six NBA championships with Jordan at the helm.

It was one of the defining moments that shaped my outlook on life. His successful acrobatic shot, in particular, holds more meaning than just a wow moment. Jordan, when faced with an obstacle, adversity or challenge, adjusted. He didn't pass on the challenge and give up the ball. He didn't panic. He simply adjusted in midair. Most of the extraordinary shots in Jordan's career weren't contrived – they just happened as a result of the environment or pressure put upon him. Something shifted in me that night; perhaps as much as wonderment, my perspective on obstacles and challenges. I didn't fully realize it then, but now do. I was inspired and I fell in love with the game of basketball. Throughout junior high and high school I was an avid Chicago Bulls fan. We didn't have a team in Kansas City and were able to watch the Bulls games on a local television station out of Chicago called WGN. I followed the team, read Jordan's books and tried to apply his work ethic, not so much to my development as an athlete, but to the overarching philosophy of how I governed my life.

When I read that Jordan had been cut from his high school team it reminded me of flunking kindergarten and trying to overcome the setback. His story encouraged me and strengthened my drive to do everything possible to succeed. In the back of my mind I set a personal goal. While I knew I didn't have the natural talent to play basketball professionally (that growth spurt in fifth grade proved to be short lived), I wanted to be involved with or work for an NBA team. I played basketball throughout school, but the desire to work and be part of a team became something that I wanted very much to accomplish.

Political Conventions of 1992

Another defining moment came during the last night of the 1992 National Republican Convention. It was an election year and President G.H. Bush was running for reelection against the youthful and charismatic Arkansas Governor Bill Clinton. Up until that time I wasn't really into politics, but again stumbled upon the convention broadcast during a night of channel surfing. It was the last night of the convention at the Astrodome in Houston, Texas. As the former president was giving his acceptance speech, I was introduced to the political process for the first time and I took an interest. As the balloons dropped from the ceiling, signaling the end of a dramatic acceptance speech for the Republican Party's candidate for president of the United States, my interest in politics, servant leadership and national priorities began. Bush went on to lose his reelection bid to President Clinton – but something inside me sparked. I began to develop my passion for politics and leadership through service.

I became more involved in student government, serving as a representative in eighth grade, class president in grades nine through eleven, eventually running for student council president during my senior year. Politics became a real passion of mine – maybe not so much the politics part, but leadership and governing. The process and different opportunities for service all intrigued me.

Lucas Goes to Washington!

Our church youth group took a trip to the East Coast during the summer of 1996 and Washington D.C. was on the itinerary. Then-Senator John Ashcroft met our band of about 30 teenage kids on the west steps of the Capitol to impart his wisdom on the issues of the day before we went on a Capitol tour. We watched a debate take place on the Senate floor from the gallery up above and I realized how zeroed in I was on what the senators were discussing. Some of the group saw the tour as a boring "filler of time" or necessary history lesson, but I took it all in. I wanted to return to Washington D.C. Later that evening, our bus parked a few blocks away from the 16th block of Pennsylvania Avenue, I ran south through Lafayette Park toward an exciting destination on the other side. There it stood – the most recognizable house on the face of the planet. As we all took photos and looked through the black iron gate to the North Portico of the White House, I was determined to be on the other side one day. I wanted to work there. With all my heart I wanted to work at the White House. With no contacts, no real knowledge of the national political scene, I didn't really consider how hard that might be. And as a young, idealistic teenager, I didn't much care. I dreamed just like Mom told me to do. And the seed of desire began to grow.

Looking back I laugh at how "naïve" I was. In front of the Eisenhower Executive Office Building (EEOB) there was a magnolia tree. It was in full bloom. I borrowed a pocketknife from one of our chaperones, David Nickerson, reached over the black iron fence and cut off a flower to give to my friend, Havilah Bruders. No one would dare try such a thing now, in the years since September 11, 2001. I guess it goes to show what one can accomplish with no guile, stupidity and a little crush. Havi would later return the favor by giving me an old photo of the White House that she found. I placed the photo on my locker during senior year of high school to remind myself of the dream – to return to Washington D.C. and work at the White House.

A Night at the Movies

The next summer (1997) after our church youth trip to Washington D.C., the feature film *Air Force One* was released with actor Harrison Ford as the lead. Ford portrayed a president who was on Air Force One when it was hijacked by terrorists. The movie was released in late July and I could barely contain my excitement. With my dear friend Megan Noland and a group of other friends, I cheered on "President James Marshall" as he re-took his plane, defeated the terrorists, and saved his wife and family.

The movie was screened by then-President Bill Clinton. On the big screen it seemed like Air Force One was a colossal house. Hollywood has its way of making things seem larger than they are, which caused me to wonder, *Is it really that big?* I wondered if there really was an escape pod, a large conference room, presidential quarters and state-of-the-art communications equipment to allow a president to run a war from the plane if he had to. I had never seen Air Force One up close – only on TV and now the big screen. As I watched the movie with my friends the seed of another dream was hatched: *I wanna fly on that plane.* I filed the wish away; having no idea how few people ever received the enormous privilege of travelling in such a way.

Three Dreams

Looking back, I have to admit I was more than a bit naïve, but the seeds were planted and what took root were three dreams, three big goals that dominated my thoughts and propelled me towards the future. I learned that without guile, but with a lot of heart, hard work, and grace, goals can be achieved. As I finished high school, I began to prepare for the next phase of life and thought about how the next 10-20 years would unfold. I was all over the map in what I wanted to be and in what I wanted to accomplish. It was extremely important to me to be a servant leader and share my testimony of Christ and His grace in my life. I wanted to travel to Africa for ministry and to continue trying to make an impact in church and youth ministry. The desire to go to college was there, too, and I made those preparations through the requisite tests, applications and visits to colleges across the country. With all of those important "check the box" steps in mind, the more whimsical, some would say, less practical goals didn't lie dormant. My dreams were very much alive. The end result didn't play out exactly like I envisioned, but I can honestly say it turned out better than all my planning.

After graduation Mom pulled me aside and asked me, "What's next?" and what I wanted to do with my life. I expressed to her a variety of goals, but the three dreams in particular. I told her I wanted to work for the NBA, fly on Air Force One, and work at the White House. I also expressed my desire to travel and share my testimony of Christ. *Faith, politics and sports?* Mom must have thought I had lost my mind, but she always seemed to believe in me more than I believed in myself. Believing in your children is one of those top ten rules of being a good parent, I suppose. Her advice was as it had always been: to remember who I am and who I represent and that if I put my mind to it – I could accomplish anything.

I had no idea what the next ten years would reveal or the grace, hard work, resourcefulness and faith that would be required. I never imagined I would travel to Oaxaca, Mexico to share my testimony of Jesus Christ and teach young students English. I never thought I would be blessed to play soccer with new-found friends halfway around the world in Kigali, Nigeria. Then, there was the trip to Nairobi, Kenya. I was never more at peace than when I walked along the rocky beach of Lake Victoria in east central Africa with an 82 year-old man who had made a decision for Jesus Christ. He leaned upon me for support as we walked far enough out into the lake so he could be baptized.

And then there was an incredible internship, the chance of a lifetime to work on a presidential campaign, serve the nation while working at the White House, the incredible grace to fly aboard Air Force One, followed by the opportunity to make a positive impact towards social change in the community while working for an NBA team.

There were times of doubt to be sure; times of hardship, disappointment and moments when I almost gave up. In the final analysis, however, I felt a strong desire to keep going and to never give up. There was always that assurance that God would "show me something" and everything would be all right. I believed that if I kept adjusting, propelling forward and taking action, the end result would be better than all my planning. While none of my life goals or big-time dreams had any common thread, each experience built upon itself and prepared me to receive the next blessing. The skill sets acquired for one goal lent themselves as preparation and a foundation to step into the next opportunity. I matured with each challenge, met each obstacle, and survived each storm. And with God's help I will continue to do so.

I encourage you to reflect on the story of the three trees and remind yourself to keep going and be patient. Adjust, shift in the air like Michael Jordan used to when he met challenges. If you continue to take action and move forward, God's going to show you something: the larger purpose. It may not turn out exactly as you plan, but I promise the conclusion will be better than all of your planning.

CHAPTER SIX

THE VALUE OF PREPARATION

Talent alone won't make you a success. Neither will being in the right place at the right time, unless you are ready. The most important question is: Are you ready?
—Johnny Carson

Eight Months in Mexico

After graduation, I struggled with the push and pull of all my dreams and the need to "check the box" with higher education and other pursuits. I was offered an opportunity to travel to Mexico to study Spanish, share in ministry and teach English to elementary and middle school students. I wrestled with the need to remain involved with church endeavors and the necessity of continuing my education. I was accepted into college but as the summer of 1998 turned into fall I felt that same assurance, "Wait. I'll show you something more." I decided to trust God and go to Oaxaca, Mexico. The rest of my friends went off to college, married and began their families. I was excited, though. Nathan Sherer, my partner in crime, and I were about to embark on a unique adventure. After sending notice that I wouldn't be attending the university that year, I packed a large, blue duffel bag, large enough for me to actually climb inside, and prepared to head south of the border.

I had never been away from home for longer than a week before and had no clue what the implications of being abroad would do for my emotional and intellectual growth. We spent the next eight months (September 1998 to May 1999) in Oaxaca, Mexico. Having gone through only an introductory course in high school, I didn't know much Spanish at all. It was time to learn real fast, though – one of those sink or swim scenarios. My first day in Mexico consisted of a horrible head cold, not being able to read any signs or communicate outside of "Dónde está el baño (where is the bathroom)?" The homesickness set in almost from the start. I was soon on the phone to my mom telling her what a gigantic mistake I had made. She was quick to point out the greater meaning. "Tough times are training grounds for the good times," she said. In other words, "Buck up kid! And stop whining!"

During the bus ride from the Texas border down to Oaxaca I became ill. I was sneezing uncontrollably when a young Hispanic man went to the bathroom and brought me back a whole roll of toilet paper. Not knowing how to say anything else I stammered, "Gracias," and looked at him with as grateful as an expression as I could muster. He waved to me a sign of understanding, "De nada," and went back to his seat.

The next eight months proved to be extremely challenging but immensely rewarding. I entered a foreign territory, a whole new world and phase of life. I was miserable to begin with. I was also scared, not knowing what to expect, and as homesick as I was actually physically sick. But Mom was, as always, pretty spot on with her advice. If I was going to achieve my dreams I had to go through the preparation and training ground of personal development. The lesson is this: sometimes preparation is hard, grueling, and painful, but any goal worth lasting value will require sacrifice in order to achieve it. I would never be developed enough or ready enough to take advantage of the goals I sought without preparation, and I think that's true for all of us.

I came to appreciate the brief time I spent in Mexico. It was the "boot camp" I needed to mature.

> *Any goal worth lasting value will require sacrifice in order to achieve it.*

I enrolled in a school to learn Spanish, *Instituto Cultural De Oaxaca* and was thrown into the deep end within my first week. The funny thing is, while I didn't speak Spanish – my teacher didn't speak any English. I felt like a child, learning to walk again for the first time. September and October 1998 were excruciating months dedicated to vocabulary drills, learning verb conjugations, and attempting to hold a basic conversation. Once I learned the language, though, life became a lot easier. For example, I could finally explain, in Spanish, to the gentlemen at the barber shop how I wanted my hair cut – a hi-skin fade. It was downright comedic trying to communicate the desired haircut before. With a little knowledge under my belt, I wasn't fluent, but at least I was able to communicate the basics; muy corte arriba y calva en el lado. Roughly translated that means very short on top and bald on the sides!

Three times a week, my buddy Nathan Sherer and I would travel by bus 45 minutes east to a little town called Mitla. We would visit our friends and share in ministry. Every Friday we'd challenge a few of the locals who became our very good friends to a game of pickup basketball. What always struck me was a young lady in her twenties by the name of Minerva. Nathan and I thought we had the upper hand because she would show up with a dress on and flat-heeled dress shoes. But she could shoot the lights out and was pretty adept at boxing us out, too. Some might have thought it was a friendly game of pickup. After all, we didn't have the normal trappings of a standard court. We played on a cement slab with a barely recognizable three-point line, with equally faded free throw markings. The rim had no net and was slightly bent, but it still reminded me of home. Our battles on the court could have been billed as the NBA Finals, the intensity level was so high. My friends liked to win as much as I did.

I enjoyed the basketball, but the time that was the most rewarding was spent teaching English to the neighborhood kids. Ranging anywhere from third grade to young adults in high school, everyone was eager to learn. We would gather at the town's community center after school around 4:00 to learn the basics and get to know each other's culture. They were enthusiastic to talk to a black guy from America, as well. There weren't many people who looked like me visiting the small rural town of Mitla, Mexico. In fact, there wasn't anybody else like me. Every week we would all settle in for some new vocabulary lessons, and basic conversation. It was a pretty fair trade. I would teach them the basics of English vocabulary and they helped me with my Spanish. Some of the kids sacrificed their regular academics to come and learn. They also learned English in school and told me their teachers graded them harder on their schoolwork because they were learning additional English from an American. The children said the teachers thought they had an unfair advantage. If the teachers only knew! Yet the class, and our time together, was open to anyone who wanted to come and learn.

College Bound

I returned home to Independence, Missouri a week before my birthday in May and by July 4, I found myself in Nigeria on another mission trip. A month later, in the fall of 1999, I began my studies at the University of Central Missouri. In college, I soon settled on political science and speech communication as areas of focus. My political science professor, Dr. Gregg Gunderson, provided a whole new depth of understanding to international relations. It was during his class that we conducted a mock simulation of the United Nations. The class was divided into groups, each representing a country throughout the world. Dr. Gunderson would act as "God" by impacting each of our nation states with events out of our control – crises, and terrorist attacks. We learned the art of diplomacy, how to trade, who to trust among our allies and how to navigate an extremely complex world while protecting our sovereignty and national interests. Whether our decisions and national policies went according to plan depended on the depth of our research and the quality of our plans as well as the strength of our imaginations and proposals, combined with a little luck of the dice. Dr. Gunderson, playing God, would roll the dice and anything over a five meant our alliances, trade deals, elections, or even covert operations, were a success. Anything less and…you guessed it – set back, disease, hurricanes, storms and other acts of nature that we would need to deal with.

In one particular instance we had to launch a covert operation into another country to extract American citizens being held hostage. We had to do this while not causing an international incident with a rogue ally. It was untenable to launch all-out war. So team USA concocted a covert plan in painstaking detail, with as much plausibility as possible to free the hostages. The plan had to be airtight in order to pass the threshold for a successful mission. The better the plan, the lower the number on the dice we could receive and still be successful. We would learn about "world events" and the success or failure of the different countries' endeavors through the class paper that Dr. Gunderson would release at the beginning of each period. Dr. Gunderson's international relations class fueled a passion and interest for contemporary affairs and world events.

A New Millennium, a New President

Fall of 2000 brought us the first presidential election of the new millennium. As the election season unfolded, I watched with intense interest. It was the first time I would be eligible to vote and I was excited to fulfill my civic duty. It was the end of President Bill Clinton's two terms in office. This election would pit the two-term governor of Texas, George W. Bush, against Vice President Al Gore, Clinton's heir apparent. I followed the election with interest that only burned brighter as election-day drew near and the post-election drama wore on.

On Tuesday, Nov. 7, I remember driving along highway 50 between Warrensburg, Missouri and Independence to vote for the first time. The designated precinct and place to vote was the site of my elementary school, Thomas Hart Benton. What made the process all the more special is that our elderly neighbor, Mary Beck, was a poll adviser. Her nickname was "Missy B." She became our family "Grandma for all Occasions," coming to school on Grandparents Day, standing in as the grandmother when some of my brothers and sisters married, going to graduations, loaning some of us her car to take our driving tests in, and teaching us how to play card games were a few of Missy B's jobs, but believe me there were many more slots she filled in our lives. Mom couldn't have made it without Missy B, and now here she was, helping me through the process of voting for the first time. I was excited, but I was also in unfamiliar territory. Missy B to the rescue!

In January, I watched the inauguration of the new president on television. It seemed that the themes and messages throughout spoke not just to America's promise, but to the individual struggles of my life. Then President Bush said, "That everyone belongs, that everyone deserves a chance, and that no insignificant person was ever born." His words, "The ambitions of some Americans are limited by failing schools and hidden prejudice and the circumstances of their birth," struck an unmistakable chord in my heart. He exhorted the nation to appreciate diversity and embrace personal responsibility. He encouraged us to serve our nation, beginning with our neighbor and asked us to "be citizens that build communities of service and a nation of character." His words turned a key inside of me and unlocked a door. It was the last few paragraphs of this inaugural speech, however, that lit a fire inside of me and reminded me of the dreams lying dormant within. He closed with these words:

After the Declaration of Independence was signed, Virginia statesman John Page wrote to Thomas Jefferson: "We know the race is not to the swift nor the battle to the strong. Do you not think an angel rides in the whirlwind and directs this storm?" We are not this story's Author, who fills time and eternity with His purpose. Yet His purpose is achieved in our duty, and our duty is fulfilled in service to one another. Never tiring, never yielding, never finishing, we renew that purpose today, to make our country more just and generous, to affirm the dignity of our lives and every life. This work continues. The story goes on. And an angel still rides in the whirlwind and directs this storm.

Encouragement from a Mentor

Outside of my mother, there were few people I looked up to growing up who compared to John and Lori Perry. This dynamic duo was a team of intellect, faith, drive, ambition and incredible kindness. I was extremely close to their daughter Megan throughout high school and thought of her as family. As academic pursuits collided with the need to sustain myself financially, the Perrys graciously allowed me a place in their home during college. I commuted to college with Megan and her affable and quick witted husband, Derek, twice a week. The other three days, I held down a part-time job at a vitamin distribution warehouse and officiated basketball and volleyball to make ends meet. My last two years in college, except for my final semester, were spent at the Perry home. They took me in as part of their family and encouraged me to go after my life goals.

Lori, especially, noticed my passion for politics and interest in world affairs. One evening during the summer of 2001 she came home from a business trip and told me of an encounter on the plane ride with a man who worked for Congressman J.C. Watts of Oklahoma. Watts was a conservative African American who had risen to leadership within the U.S. House of Representatives and I had followed his path of service. I'm honored to say I would later give him and his wife a tour of the West Wing; one of the many highlights of my time at the White House. Lori mentioned my ambitions to this man and described my interest in politics. She asked him for advice on how to get my foot in the door. He gave Lori some pointers, which she, in turn, passed along.

I had the desire to get involved with politics, but not a lot of knowledge about how to make it a reality. An internship was required as part of the credit hours towards my political science degree, so I began to plan for an internship at the state capital in Jefferson City, Missouri. Dr. Shari Garber-Bax, a former political science professor at the University of Central Missouri, stood ready to facilitate an internship at the state capital, but Lori encouraged me to dream bigger and embrace the moment of opportunity. As I began to heed her counsel, an alternative course of action began to unfold for the spring semester of 2002. I went online and began researching internships in Washington

D.C. in August of 2001. I came across the Washington Center for Academic Internships and Seminars. I submitted my application and was accepted into their Diversity Leaders program. As part of the process the Washington Center sent my application and materials out to a number of organizations and agencies in the D.C. area. There were two places I specifically asked the Washington Center to send my resume for consideration of an internship: the office of Congressman J.C. Watts and the White House.

Tuesday September 11, 2001

Most everyone of age to understand remembers where he or she was and what they were doing when they first heard the news that September morning. I had finished my morning workout at the Blue Springs YMCA and was headed down highway 7 towards school when my friend Robby Baber reached me on my cell phone to tell me that a plane hit a building in New York. I immediately turned the radio on for the rest of the drive. As it became clear what had taken place, a sense of incredible sadness, followed by anger became the seesaw of emotion that followed over the next few days. When I arrived at school I went to history class as scheduled, but expected that class would be cancelled. What I found was a mix of ambivalence toward what had occurred. I don't know whether the gravity of what had taken place failed to sink in because the professor announced that while all had probably heard of the unfortunate accident in New York and while it was indeed sad, we needed to continue with our studies. By then the second plane had crashed into the second tower. Along with countless others, I sensed that it was no accident. I raised my hand, stood and with a mix of resolve and anger blurted out, "It was an attack and the United States will destroy the guys who did this!" I actually used more colorful language to describe the "guys," which I apologized to the class for later that week. After my emotional outburst the class was stunned. A few gave me encouraging glances, but no one dared to challenge the professor, who obviously wanted to move forward with her lesson plan of the hour. I found it oddly ironic that we would "learn about American history" while one of the most historic days in American history unfolded right before us. I sat back down, but after about three more minutes of biting my tongue I stood up and said, "I'm sorry, I gotta go. I can't just sit here" and proceeded to march out of class. Looking back, it's a wonder I got an A in that class after such blatant defiance. Given the circumstances, though, and the enormity of that day and the impact it had on our country, I'm hopeful the professor understood.

I went to my friend Nathan Harris' dorm room and was glued to the television for the rest of the day. We huddled around the television and watched the replay of the Twin Towers collapse over and over. No one knew quite what it meant and the reports of other attacks drew us all a little closer. I remember trying to drive back to Independence that night. I drove to the gas station only to find long lines leading up to the pump. The line to get gas stretched for four and five blocks. It seemed like fear had gripped the tiny town of Warrensburg. I could only imagine the same scene was unfolding in many towns across the nation. I gave up trying to get gas after the third gas station I visited had the same long lines.

September 11th was a searing experience for me, as it was for so many across our nation. Lori was in New Jersey and we could not get a hold of her to find out whether she was OK because all of the cell phone towers were overwhelmed. We found out later that she had planned to visit the World Trade Center with a friend that day, but it didn't work out. Over the next few days and months I tried to heal along with the rest of the country.

A resolve and desire to go to Washington took hold of my heart. I wanted to do something. I considered joining the military, even visited the local ROTC on campus to get information. My friends who knew of my desire to serve cautioned me to withdraw my application to go to D.C., saying it was too dangerous. They couldn't believe that while others were doing their best to get away from the nation's capital that I still wanted to go. But I wasn't swayed. In my heart I could think of no better time than the present to travel, serve the country and do my small part. I could only donate so much blood, pray or send money. It was time to go. It was time to volunteer whatever I could, for just a short time; to do the things I believed were worth sacrificing for.

An Improbable Internship

The Washington Center for Academic Seminars and Internships informed me that the White House was strongly considering not having interns for the next semester after 9/11. I was disappointed but I still held out hope that I would be able to go to D.C. and fulfill my dream while serving during a time of great consequence. The matter wasn't helped any when some of my friends, who thought it their duty, tried to dampen my optimism. Well meaning, they sought to lower my expectations and "protect my feelings" by boldly predicting that it probably wouldn't work out, and even if the White House did end up accepting interns the chances that I would make the cut were slim. They were logical, I guess, in their predictions. They said, "Lucas, come on! Really? How could you ever get an internship there? You don't know anybody. You don't have any connections. It's only for rich people, or students who go to top colleges and universities." Subtle mentions of my family connections were meant to remind me of where I came from. I was the son of a woman who traded sexual favors for alcohol and drugs. For some, that reality alone was enough to predict and pronounce my ambition a failure.

I was not without doubt myself. I had heard the White House internship program was only for Ivy Leaguers and the well connected, but I hoped against all odds and believed, perhaps naïvely, that it would work out for the best. I learned later that the White House receives anywhere between 1,000 to 2,000 applications for internships each semester. On average, they typically choose about a hundred to fill the available slots. So the odds of getting an internship, for someone like me, with no family connections, relationships, or official ties to a specific political party were pretty slim.

I received a call from Congressman Watt's office in early November about the possibility of coming to D.C. and working on Capitol Hill. I was thrilled by the opportunity. After a 30-minute phone interview I was more excited than ever to travel to D.C. I received a call back after Thanksgiving offering me the position. I hadn't heard from the White House and feared that either I didn't make the cut or that internships were not going to be filled that semester.

Andrea McDaniel from the Office of Personnel at the White House called me on a frigid winter morning in late December 2001. I was at work when she called, so my colleagues had the pleasure of seeing me turn "white as a ghost" when the intercom in the warehouse squawked and the receptionist said "Lucas, you have a call on line two…umm… it's Andrea McDaniel from the White House." My heart leapt in my chest and my stomach did a number of somersaults as I walked towards the back of the warehouse to take the call. Andrea told me that my resume had come across her desk and then she apologized for calling so late in the process. They had just decided to accept interns for the next semester. I don't remember the interview at all. I was too shell shocked by the fact that the White House had just called.

I had two more phone interviews before Andrea called back in early January to offer me the position as one of the interns for Ed Moy, special assistant to the president for personnel. Moy's bio was and remains impressive. He was responsible for "recommending candidates for the most senior of political appointments for 11 Cabinet Departments and cabinet-rank agencies in the human services, natural resources, legal, and national security fields." Additionally, he was responsible for senior political appointments for 32 independent federal agencies. The wide array of agencies included the Social Security Administration, Federal Energy Regulatory Commission, National Labor Relations Board, and the National Endowment for the Arts. He even served on the panel responsible for the U.S. Department of Homeland Security transition. He later served as director of the U.S. Mint. I reached out to Congressman J.C. Watt's office to explain the opportunity to serve at the White House and, thankfully, they understood. I had no idea what the next chapter in my life would bring. I didn't choose the office of personnel. I had wanted to serve in the communications or political affairs office. But God showed once again that he is in absolute control. It proved to be another lesson or testament to the phrase "better than all your planning." I thought being chosen and getting the opportunity to be 1 of 100 young students to serve at the White House in the spring of 2002 was the fulfillment of my dream to work at the White House. I had no idea just what God would do and how the following few months would literally shape the next five years of my life.

My first day of work as an intern was on Monday, January 21, 2002. I took the metro (or subway) located on the orange line, six stops from Ballston station to Farragut West. I came up the escalator on the 17th Street side when I should have exited on the 18th Street side and proceeded to get lost. This was embarrassing, because I practiced the route the day before. I knew the White House was to the north and the building I would work in, 1800 G street, was to the northwest. So I started north and crossed over H Street and through Lafayette Park. As I crossed Lafayette Park, I recalled doing the same thing a few years before. There it was again. The last time I was in that spot, on Pennsylvania Avenue, was in 1996, during the church caravan trip and now I was back. I stood silently for a moment thanking God for the development, determination, and preparation that had brought me to that moment. After thanking Him for the privilege and opportunity to fulfill my dream I took a quick photo, turned right towards 1800 G Street and began an incredible journey.

At six weeks old with Mom.

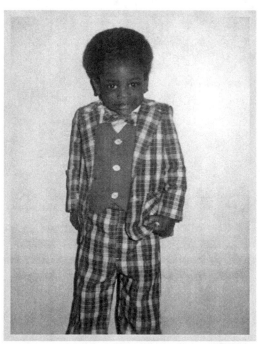

Adoption Day March 17, 1982. I was a few months shy of turning three and decked out in mom's specially purchased J.C. Penny suit!

A super mom with her 11 children. We are a diverse and happy family. I was 6 years old.

On the steps of the capitol with church youth group in 1996 with former Senator and U.S. Attorney General John Ashcroft.

Making breakfast on a mission trip in Kenya April 2000.

First time meeting the President
March 25, 2002 (6 months after 9/11).
Courtesy of the George W. Bush Presidential Library

Mom, Dad and I with former President George W. Bush.
Trip home to Kansas City Missouri February 1, 2008.
Courtesy of Reflections Photography

Me and my dear friends and White House Colleagues
Jason Recher and Jared Weinstein at Mitt Romney's house May 2008.
Courtesy of Reflections Photography

Checking my blackberry on a military helicopter over Salt Lake City Utah in May 2008.
I'm wearing earplugs because of the noise.
Courtesy of the George W. Bush Presidential Library

Looking out the window of a military helicopter.
Courtesy of the George W. Bush Presidential Library

On Air Force One with former President George W. Bush, Senior Advisor Barry Jackson, and Attorney General Jon Bruning en route to Omaha Nebraska December 2007.

Courtesy of the George W. Bush Presidential Library

July 18, 2008 departing Air Force One for the last time during the Bush Administration. Last flight before moving to Florida to work for the Orlando Magic seven days later.

Courtesy of the George W. Bush Presidential Library

Departure photo with former President George W. Bush in January 2009.
This was a few weeks before he left office.
Courtesy of the George W. Bush Presidential Library

Presenting former President George W. Bush with a personalized Orlando Magic jersey.
Courtesy of the George W. Bush Presidential Library

Departure photo with former President George W. Bush in January 2009.
In the Oval Office telling the president about my new job with the Orlando Magic.
Courtesy of the George W. Bush Presidential Library

At center court watching a Community Relations Department presentation.
Photo Credit: Orlando Magic Photographer Gary Bassing

*At center court for a presentation with Orlando Magic Game
Presentation Manager Karly Skladany AKA "Headset girl."*

Photo Credit: Orlando Magic Photographer Fern Medina

*Presenting an Orlando Magic jersey to Michael Steele, Chairman of the
Republican National Committee (RNC) at center court before a Magic game.*

Photo Credit: Orlando Magic Photographer Fern Medina

NBA Simulation Game to open Amway Center September 2010.

Photo Credit: Orlando Magic Photographer Fern Medina

NBA Simulation Game to open Amway Center September 2010.
With former players Nick Anderson, Bo Outlaw and Orlando Magic CEO Bob Vander Weide.
Photo Credit: Orlando Magic Photographer Fern Medina

Noche Latina "Latin Night" at Amway Arena March 2010. This was the launch
of our El Magic retail line for the Hispanic Community. Pictured are Orlando Magic
Vice President of Community Relations Linda Landman Gonzalez and
President of the Hispanic Chamber of Commerce of Metro Orlando Ramon Ojeda.
Photo Credit: Orlando Magic Photographer Gary Bassing

December 2010 on court at Amway Center with two of my mentors, President of the Magic Alex Martins and Vice President of Communications Joel Glass.

Photo Credit: Orlando Magic Photographer Fern Medina

CHAPTER SEVEN

MEETING THE PRESIDENT

The true measure of a man is how he treats someone who can do him absolutely no good.
—Dr. Samuel Johnson

This is the final test of a gentleman: his respect for those who can be of no possible value to him.
—William Lyon Phelps, Author and Scholar

An Ordinary Monday Turns Extraordinary

Monday, March 25, 2002 was pretty much business as usual until after lunch. I thought it was just going to be another Monday in the office, but I was mistaken. Spring was just setting in on the nation's capital and I had no idea that when I went to work on that day it would prove to be such a pivotal moment in my life. I had just returned from lunch and was settling in for some afternoon research on possible candidates to serve on a board that would be appointed by the president. I had literally just sat down at my desk when the director for the intern program, Mike Sanders, came around the corner. He dispensed with the usual pleasantries and got straight to the point. He said, "Lucas, someone's going to call you and they are going to ask you to be part of something. I can't tell you what it is right now, but my advice to you is to say yes." As a wide-eyed 22-year-old intern, my first inclination was to always follow orders. What was an intern to do other than that? I didn't realize at the time that out of about 100 interns working at the White House, Mr. Sanders had recommended me to participate in a photo opportunity for *Parade Magazine* ... with the president. Having no clue as to what was about to take place, my response was an enthusiastic, "Yes sir." Not knowing what, where, how, or when, I trusted that Mike wouldn't steer me wrong.

Fifteen minutes later, I got a call from the USA Freedom Corps office. The Freedom Corps was an organization formed by the president in response to the 9/11 attacks and announced during his annual State of the Union Address on January 29, 2002. Former President George W. Bush called for "every American to commit at least two years, 4,000 hours over the rest of our lifetimes to the service of our neighbors and our country." The purpose of the Freedom Corps was to "sustain and extend the best that has emerged in America" and its focus was three fold: "Responding in case of crisis at home; rebuilding our communities; and extending American compassion throughout the world." In practice, this new initiative would serve to strengthen the foundation of Americorps, the Peace Corps and the Senior Corps with one overarching goal: to respond to the terrorist attacks not only with justice, but with an increased level of service and kindness to show, by example, the best of who we were as Americans.

Having a brief synopsis of the program explained to me, I was told that they asked Mike Sanders if there was an intern he would recommend to take part in this photo opportunity and he suggested me. They asked if I would be willing to participate and I remembered

Mike's (who is now a state representative in Oklahoma) counsel to me. I accepted without hesitation.

First Time in the West Wing

The Freedom Corps office had me rush over to the West Wing where I was met and promptly told to remove my suit coat and tie. They gave me a blue Freedom Corps t-shirt to wear instead and ushered me through the West Wing to the South Lawn. I couldn't believe it – even as it was happening. I recalled how back in high school I had peered through heavy reinforced black iron gates from the street towards the West Wing on the church youth trip. It was that day that I settled in my mind that I wanted to be on the inside and it was happening right then and there – as sure as I breathed.

The West Wing was built in 1902 out of necessity. Teddy Roosevelt had six children and the business of the country was accomplished on the second story of the Executive Mansion we commonly refer to as the White House. With all of the children, there just wasn't enough room for him and his staff to conduct the nation's business and run a large family, so he decided to build more space. The end result, over two more renovations, was a small three-story, modest structure that has come to represent the most powerful and influential office space on the face of the earth. And I'm not exaggerating! The West Wing is home base for the president and senior administration officials. It's where the Oval Office, the Press Room and the top secret Situation Room, created by John F. Kennedy after The Cuban Missile Crisis, are housed. The West Wing is a whirlwind of activity; the place where pivotal decisions are made and where history unfolds every day.

I had never before seen inside the building that houses the official office of the president and his senior staff. Well … that's not completely accurate. I followed the television series *The West Wing*, written by Aaron Sorkin, religiously. I knew the cast and characters of "President Josiah Barlett's" administration like the back of my hand and rarely missed an episode. The closest I had ever been to the Oval Office was just inside the entry on the ground floor by the phone in the lobby. My task was to pass on documents to an aide who would come from "inside" to retrieve them. I was then to leave. The rule was that you could not roam through the West Wing without an escort. And even your escort had to have a specific level of access. Not just any White House staff member could saunter through. If you didn't have a legitimate reason to be there you were encouraged by the ever-vigilant and watchful Secret Service to "keep it movin'." My friend Jeff Anger was in town from Independence that day. During lunch we had walked through the Eisenhower Executive Office Building freely. I wanted him to experience as much as he could, so we tip-toed into the waiting area on the ground floor of the West Wing like a couple of thieves in the night; as if tip toeing and acting like we shouldn't be there would help us. I had him quickly stand in front of the large presidential seal by the door for a picture. We waved to the Secret Service on the other side of the glass, I think in an attempt to convince them we should be there, and left in a hurry! Again – rookie mistake!

As I entered the double glass doors, the same doors I merely peered through just an hour before, I felt a sense of awe and reverence. It was the same entry congressmen, senators, the vice president, cabinet officials and other public officials used as an entry and exit for their businesses in the West Wing. It was such a special place and an overwhelming moment to experience. I found out quickly that the layout wasn't exactly the same as it was portrayed in the fictional NBC television show. It was a lot smaller than I had expected – like a small house.

Three Pictures to Remember

I followed my escort through the hallways on the ground floor and then up the stairs to the second floor where the Oval Office resides. As we quickly made our journey, I noticed large poster sized portraits, called "jumbos," lining the walls at about eye level. Most of the photos at this time were of the stirring moments that took place in the few months after 9/11. There were three large photos in particular that stood out.

As I passed chief White House photographer Eric Draper's office and a few national security offices, I saw a series of three photographs he had taken, all involving the president's hands. In the first one, the president was holding a police badge. It was the police shield of George Howard, a fallen Port Authority police officer in New York City who died in his attempt to rescue others from the World Trade Center. The president had visited the families of those who had lost loved ones. One person in particular was a woman in a wheel chair named Arlene Howard. She gave the president her son's police shield, which he put in his pocket and showed to the nation on September 20, 2001 during his speech to a joint session of Congress after the attacks. He told the nation that it was his "reminder of lives that ended and a task that does not end."

The second photo was of the president holding a baseball. It was taken a month after 9/11 on October 29 in the dugout at Yankee Stadium. Game three of the 2001 World Series was held in New York that year and the president went to game three to throw out the ceremonial first pitch. The Secret Service put a heavy bulletproof vest on him and he had been practicing his pitches in the dugout to get used to the new weight when Derek Jeter came by for a chat. Jeter asked the President where he was gonna throw from. Bush thought about it for a moment, considering his decreased mobility due to the extra weight he was carrying and then responded that he would probably throw from the base of the mound. Derek gave the president some sage advice that he better throw from the mound if he didn't want to get booed.

With the extra weight and decreased range of motion the president put on a blue sweater emblazoned with "FDNY," a visible salute to the New York City Fire Department and strode out to the mound. He walked to the pitcher's mound as the sold out crowd of almost 60,000 chanted, "U-S-A! U-S-A! U-S-A!" He looked up into the stands for a moment and gave the crowd, and the nation, a thumbs up. He wound up for the pitch and threw the baseball (the same baseball in the picture) right down the middle of the plate. It was a strike.

As I was escorted past the Secret Service's base of operations that sits right underneath the Oval Office, and then up the narrow carpeted stairs, there was one last picture that caught my eye. It was on the second floor landing. In this photo, the president was at the World Trade Center standing on the rubble of what was left of a scorched fire truck on September 14, 2001. He was standing with retired fire fighter Bob Beckwith at his side and a bullhorn in his hand. The president visited New York to view the damage and comfort the families of those who were lost. He decided to speak to the rescue crews and relief workers, who in some cases had driven through the night from as far as the Midwest to help with the search and recovery. They were tired and determined to try and save any who might still be caught in the wreckage. The rescue workers and volunteers had a hard time hearing his remarks and yelled, "We can't hear you!" In an unscripted –and one of the most authentic – moments to ever occur during his presidency, the former president responded in as loud a voice as he could,

"I can hear you!" The workers cheered. He continued, "I can hear you. The rest of the world hears you, and the people who knocked these buildings down will hear all of us soon!" The workers erupted into a spontaneous chant of, "U-S-A! U-S-A! U-S-A!"

The photos were of different moments during a consequential time in our nation's history, but the message and the words that came through were the same; encouragement, belief, hope, and resolve. The message was triumph over tragedy and persevering through storm and temporary defeats onto victory. We were one nation and as the poet John Donne once said, "No man is an island. No man stands alone." With a simple thumbs up a president conveyed to our country that regardless of where we had been and what we had experienced, we would get through it and be OK. The message served as an important reminder to me of the strength needed to get through any difficulty, struggle or tragedy. When I recall the images and the stories behind them, I'm reminded of a simple lesson. It applies to our individual and private lives just as much as teams, families, or the organizations and associations we belong to. If we are willing to make the decision to never be deterred from the circumstance of the moment, no matter how hard, our situations in life will never define us and effect who we ultimately want to become or what we wish to accomplish.

Those photos and more passed by my vision as I was led down the hallway and through the doors that led out to the West Colonnade. The West Colonnade is famous for the photos of former President John F. Kennedy and his brother Bobby Kennedy conferring during the Cuban missile crisis. Every president since 1902 used this walkway as a path of travel to and from the executive residence to the West Wing. Countless world leaders had traveled this vaunted walkway through every season, summer and winter, and now I was hurriedly being ushered through as well. As we strode through the Colonnade, on my right was the Rose Garden with the large floor-to-ceiling windows of the Cabinet Room overlooking the onset of spring. I was taken to the Palm Room to wait until the others who were to participate in the photo opportunity arrived. The Palm Room is a room full of plants that connects the West Colonnade and the West Wing to the Executive Mansion. I sat down on a bench and took in the smells of the various flowers and plants. I barely believed I was actually there. *I can't wait to tell Mom!* I thought. I had no idea that the day would get even better. I would have more news to phone home with.

My Freedom Corps escort came to retrieve me and I followed her to the North Gate to collect the other participants who would be in the photo. As we waited at the Northwest Appointments Gate I looked beyond the heavy black iron-gate that separated the White House complex from Pennsylvania Avenue and whispered a prayer of gratitude. Only six years before, I had been on the other side of that fence looking in. And while I knew the internship would eventually come to an end, it was neat to pretend that just for a while I was on the "inside."

A Handshake Changes a Life

Once the other "students" arrived we were on our way back up the driveway. I say "students" because other than me I think the oldest may have been about 12 years old. I was a good ten years older than the most senior of this bunch and immediately felt out of place. I knew I looked young for my age, but not this young! We were ushered up the driveway, past the Press Room and through the Palm Room again. We passed through the Rose Garden and stopped on the stone walkway that proceeds from the Oval Office to the South Lawn. The *Parade Magazine* staff began to set up their equipment for the shoot and all seemed pretty standard, if you consider hanging out on the

South Lawn of the White House pretty standard. After waiting there for a few minutes while the staff finished their preparations, I began to notice that nothing about this was at all normal. Secret Service, with their trademark dark suits, sun glasses, serious expressions and ubiquitous earpieces started appearing, seemingly out of nowhere. It then started to dawn on me that this wasn't just a photo with some school kids who were making an impact in volunteer service. It was with the president. A light bulb clicked on and my mind went into high gear, but it was a little too late. An outside door to the Oval Office swung open and President George W. Bush strode down the stone walkway towards us. With a little trepidation I mustered what courage I had to situate the children, as if pretending to be a mother hen would make me less nervous. As the kids assembled to shake hands, Bush came to me last and with a big smile on his face just stuck out his hand. "Hey, I'm George," was the president's simple greeting. "Hey... I'm Lucas," I responded. I didn't really know what else to say. I was a definite rookie having never met any celebrity – let alone the president! – before.

It was then that my nervousness melted away. It was because of the president. I can honestly say that it was easier meeting the president for the first time than it is being at a nightspot on a Friday evening and trying to initiate a conversation with a girl. It was because of how he interacted not just with me but with all the kids. He started joking with us and dispensing advice as we began to walk down the cobble path towards a swing. All the while the *Parade Magazine* photographer was clicking away. Being that the oldest besides me was about 12, the President and I struck up a conversation and proceeded throughout the rest of the photo shoot to just kind of "shoot the bull." He asked me where I grew up, what my goals were, where I worked in the White House and for whom. Noticing a putting green a few yards away I asked the president if he golfed much. He said he loved golf, but since

9/11 hadn't had a lot of time to indulge in that activity. He didn't feel like golfing when he had sent soldiers into battle. What would their parents think to see him out swinging the clubs when their loved ones were in harm's way protecting the homeland at his direction?

He reminisced about the swing that served as a prop for the photos. He told us he visited the South Lawn and that very swing with his twin girls when his dad, George Herbert Walker Bush, was president. Now, he was president and his girls were in their twenties and in college. He then gave us a piece of advice. He said, "Always follow your mother's advice and do what she tells you." This was more for the younger ones in the group, but it was nonetheless a good nugget of wisdom. Then he cracked a smile. "I followed my mom's advice and I became president."

The *Parade Magazine* photographer began to wind down and I assumed the photo shoot was over. I stepped aside and as I did so the President gestured to me, "Come on, let's take a personal photo." He called his official photographer, Eric Draper, over. Overcome with excitement, I unwittingly threw my arm around the president and produced a smile that could have stretched from Washington D.C. to my hometown of Independence, Missouri. An obvious breach of protocol, but being a complete novice at "celebrity meetings" as I was, I didn't know I had just committed a huge *faux pas*. I would never do that today, but the president seemed to take it in stride and leaned in for the photo. After taking the photo I turned to President Bush, knowing that the responsibilities of his office during a critical time were immense, and in reference to the post 9/11 actions in Afghanistan I told him, "Sir, the cause is just." Those were my parting words. His response was a little halting at first. He kind of took a step back, looked me in the eye and said, "Thank you, it is."

That was it. The president thanked everyone, took a few more photos and walked back into his office for the next appointment on his schedule. And just as quickly, the Secret Service and additional White House staff vanished as well. I was taken back to the Palm Room to wait while the students were taken back to the North Gate for departure.

As I sat and waited on my escort I replayed the events that had taken place. Something shifted inside of me as the entire experience made its full impact and tears came to my eyes. I whispered a prayer of thanks to God for making such an experience possible. It was better than all my planning and more than I could have ever hoped for from the internship experience.

I went back to my office and the first call I made was home to Mom. I was pumped! If Facebook and Twitter had been in existence back then I'm certain the experience would have made its way into a status update. I thought that was it – a wonderful experience and nothing else that I could always keep with me. And it was that, but more as well. The next day my boss, Ed Moy, came back to our office from a personnel meeting with the president in the Oval Office. I remember him walking down the hall towards me and his first words were, "You made a real impression on the president yesterday." I got this sinking feeling and recalled how I had inadvertently put my arm around the president like we were old chums and thought to myself, *Pack your bags buddy, the internship is over.* I imagined the Secret Service reporting the breach of protocol and exuberance and I was momentarily crestfallen. I began to apologize and he flashed me a smile and said, "What are you apologizing for?" He then told me his experience in the Oval Office a few minutes before. Moy said after the meeting the president called him aside and said, "Hey, I met this kid on the South Lawn yesterday. He said he works for you. What's his name again?" Moy replied "Lucas." "Yeah, well I really enjoyed meeting him." Moy replied back, "Probably not as much as he enjoyed meeting you, sir." The president laughed and asked, "What's his story?" Moy told him a little bit about me, my background and growing up being adopted, etc. and the president replied, "Well what can we do for him? Let's bring him on board."

Be Ready, Be Authentic, and Have Character

When Ed Moy told me this story, I was stunned. I don't remember displaying an extra degree of confidence or commanding maturity to warrant catching the president's attention. He was intensely busy and the photo opportunity was but a blip during an otherwise whirlwind of a day during a time of war. It was incredible to fathom, but it hammered home another piece of advice my mother always tried to instill in me, "Someone is always watching." The lesson was two-fold. One: I was an example of good in the world and it was important to never let people down by being less than who I could be. Two: The underlying call to action was to always bring my A game because you never know when someone might notice and be in a position to help you. Others have said, success in life, to a degree, is about relationships. If I hadn't brought my A game and worked hard in school, would I have even been an intern? If I hadn't taken my mother's advice and been at the White House early every day, engaged in seminars and proactive in the discharge of my responsibilities, would the director of interns, Mike Sanders, had ever recommended me for the chance to participate in that photo? I think we know the answer to both questions is, "Of course not."

Life can change in the blink of an eye. For me, it took about ten minutes during the course of an otherwise routine photo op and a brief handshake on the South Lawn with the leader of the free world. That day changed my life and the experience crystallized my optimism for what was possible, if only we dare to give our very best in every circumstance and situation we face. I mentioned previously that I'm a firm believer that amazing things can happen when grace meets opportunity. The grace comes from above, but you have to be prepared for the opportunity. You have to trust that someone someday is looking to catch you doing something right, so always seek to do what is right. You have to be ready, and always know that someone is watching.

The second lesson, while simple, has more power than you would think in a world where everyone is pretending, putting up walls, hiding their true agendas. We all have masks we use to protect our egos, but I learned that "keepin' it real" or being who you are is always the best policy. I know what you're going to say. If I don't have a mask people won't like me. Trust me; I've communicated that same type of garbage to myself. A few thoughts to take to heart: be authentic. I've often wondered how I made such an impression on the president that he would, in the midst of his busy life, recall a few moments on the South Lawn and have the presence of mind to remember whom I worked for and follow up with my boss. And then go one step further and ask about my story and if they could help me. I wasn't anyone important. I wasn't the chief of staff, his secretary of state or one of his senior advisors that saw him on a regular basis. I was a 22-year-old intern. I've wondered if my putting my arm around the president for the photo was so out of the ordinary that it stuck with him. That wasn't it either; although there is something there I don't want to skip over. That moment wasn't contrived in my head or rehearsed. I didn't get up that morning asking myself, *Gosh, if I ever meet the president, what would I say that would really make an impact and get his attention?* It was the knee jerk reaction of an excited kid who had just experienced something incredible, and reacted authentically in the moment. There are two reasons why I think it wasn't just a throwaway experience for him or me. One is that I was authentic and I believe he was too.

To be completely honest, I believe the implications of that experience had more to do with the president than anything I did or said. He was authentic and possessed an internal code of character that has resonated and stuck with me ever since. All of us at some point in our lives, whether it be in our families, at work, non-profit organizations or even religious institutions, will assume the responsibility of leadership. Whether it is being the head of a household, a department, corporation, a parent, or supervising an intern, we will be given the responsibility to lead. The former president taught me my first lesson in leadership that day and it is this: you know the true character of a person by how they treat the person that can do nothing for them. It's not a new concept or phrase, but the experience still drove home what author and scholar William Lyon Phelps meant. He said, "This is the final test of a gentleman: his respect for those who can be of no possible value to him." Again, I wasn't anybody important, yet he took the time to take a personal photo, had the presence of mind to remember the experience and follow up and then asked his staff if there was a place for me, if they could bring me on board. Why would anyone do that? He didn't have to. I think it was a reflection of his heart and his character – and even deeper, his respect for anyone and everyone.

Peggy Noonan, speechwriter to former President Ronald Reagan, said this about character and presidents:

> In a president, character is everything. A president doesn't have to be brilliant. He doesn't have to be clever; you can hire clever. You can hire pragmatic, and you can buy and bring in policy wonks. But you can't buy courage and decency, you can't rent a strong moral sense. A president must bring those things with him. He needs to have, in that much maligned word, but a good one nonetheless, a "vision" of the future he wishes to create. But

a vision is worth little if a president doesn't have the character,
the courage and heart, to see it through.

Ms. Noonan's words are applicable for more than just presidents. We would all do well to store for ourselves "courage and decency." If we want to be successful in business, politics, in our families and personal lives, I am wholly convinced that we must always be ready and authentic. Most importantly, our character must be unshakeable, to the point that whether our dealings are with a janitor or the president, we've resolved in our hearts to treat them one in the same.

CHAPTER EIGHT

TO EVERYTHING THERE IS A SEASON

*To everything there is a season, and a time
to every purpose under the heaven:
A time to be born, and a time to die; a time to plant, and a time to
pluck up that which is planted; A time to kill, and a time to heal;
a time to break down, and a time to build up; A time to weep, and
a time to laugh; a time to mourn, and a time to dance; A time to
cast away stones, and a time to gather stones together; a time
to embrace, and a time to refrain from embracing; A time to get,
and a time to lose; a time to keep, and a time to cast away.*
—Ecclesiastes 3:1—6

A Furious Finish to College

After my first encounter with former President Bush, I made the hard decision to return to my roots, albeit for a limited amount of time. I resolved to finish my education back home in Missouri. I thought it was important and

I owed it to Mom to complete my education before taking the next step. It was important for me personally as a symbolic victory over past obstacles and learning disabilities. I went home and in a whirlwind of credits and classes finished a little ahead of schedule so that I could return to Washington D.C. as soon as possible.

As the summer of 2003 began, Ed Moy assisted me in arranging interviews. I took a brief trip to D.C., before graduation, to begin the interview process. I was excited about the prospect of working at the Department of Justice, or Health and Human Services. One of my most memorable interviews was meeting with Matthew Hunter, who served as the White House liaison at the Department of Housing and Urban Development. They had a position open to be the personal aide to then-Secretary Mel Martinez. After my interview with Hunter he surprised me with a follow-up interview the same day with Secretary Martinez. When I met the secretary and learned of his amazing journey to become the nation's 12th HUD secretary, I decided then and there that I wanted to work at his side and learn from him. He was born in Cuba and brought to the United States as part of a relief effort. He barely spoke any English when he came here and was shuffled through two foster care homes before being reunited with his family four years later. I had an immediate connection with him and hoped to be his personal aide.

Having been an avid fan of the television show *The West Wing*, I had a pretty good idea of what being a personal aide to a top government official would entail and was excited by the opportunity. I harbored a small desire to be personal aide to the president just like Charlie on the show. Surely, this would be a great training ground. It wasn't to be, however. The phrase, "Wait, I'll show you something more," seemed to run its course again. Another interview not on my original itinerary for the trip surfaced at the last moment and took me in another direction.

During the 2002 midterm election, I did some volunteer work for then-Congressman Jim Talent. He was running for the U.S. Senate and I wanted to stay involved in politics any way I could. I helped out with research on how to make inroads into the African American community in Kansas City, Missouri and passed on contacts and connections to the leader of that effort. Through my work, Talent's field director, Joe Keatley, and I met. I kept in contact with her and sent her my resume along with a letter when I began preparing to return to D.C. My original intent was to update her on my progress in completing my studies and ask if she would be willing to serve as a reference for me. I did not know it then, but she forwarded my information to Jack Oliver, then deputy chairman of the Republican National Committee. Jack sent my information over to the president's campaign, where it landed on the desk of Terry Nelson. Nelson led the president's political and grassroots efforts critical to his re-election. I didn't understand at the time how fortuitous this random turn of events would prove to be. Terry's assistant, Jason Huntsberry, called me to set up the interview and I made the short trip across the Potomac River to a nondescript red brick office building in Arlington, Virginia. The job I interviewed for was staff assistant to the national political director. At the time, I was still focused on working for Secretary Martinez so while I was excited about the opportunity, my heart was with the Department of Housing and Urban Development.

Returning home from my trip I wondered which opportunity might unfold – hoping, wishing, praying to be able to work for Secretary Martinez. When Jason Huntsberry called me in late June to offer me the position I was excited and a little crestfallen at the same time. I asked for some time to consider the offer and he obliged with the customary 48 hours. I called Mr. Hunter in the secretary's office to see if they had made a decision. He said they were close and asked what my situation was. I was honest and told him what I had been offered, but that if the opportunity to work for the secretary presented itself, that would be my first choice. Matt gave me some heartfelt and candid advice. "You have no idea what opportunities working for the president's reelection campaign will represent," he said. He indicated it would be wise to take any opportunity that unfolded with the Bush-Cheney 2004 campaign. He told me I was a very strong candidate to be the personal aide, but that my career would be better served if I went to work on a national presidential campaign. He went on to say, "It will be a critical and historic election. Win or lose it will prove to be a formative and important life experience for you." I really, really wanted to be the secretary's personal aide so I was reluctant to take his advice at first – but am thankful I did. In December of that year Secretary Martinez resigned his Cabinet post and began a successful campaign to replace the retiring U.S. Senator Bob Graham. As it turned out, the experience proved to be better than all my planning.

I accepted the offer to work for Terry Nelson at the campaign, but first I had to complete my studies. I officially completed my course-work on Thursday July 10, 2003, was the best man in my friend Robby Baber's wedding on Saturday the 12th, flew to Washington, D.C. the Sunday morning of the 13th and began work on George W. Bush's re-election campaign the very next day, Monday July 14, 2003.

The 2004 Presidential Campaign

The 2004 campaign was an intense race filled with excitement and formative life lessons – just as Matthew Hunter predicted. Some days were better than others, but each provided a lesson and built momentum that propelled us toward election-day. It was a steady march, requiring endurance, faith, an unwavering hand, a sharp mind, and lots of caffeine. Eighteen months on a presidential campaign taught me the value of strategic planning, precise execution and to always be ready for change. It was my first real introduction to the world of politics and serving as a liaison to field offices throughout 19 target states was a baptism by fire. I was given the responsibility of managing the Bush Volunteer Program, tasked with securing over one million new volunteers for the president. I collaborated with vendors in the design, production, and distribution of campaign materials like bumper stickers, placards, yard signs, posters and novelty items. As election day drew near, I was fortunate to assist in the coordination of get-out-the-vote (GOTV) operations.

The outcome of the election came down to Florida and Ohio, just as our senior leadership team expected. In sports, as in life, the difference between winning and losing is, more often than not, a matter of inches or just a few points. It was no less true for our campaign. Election night was spent in the "war room," otherwise known as a converted conference room outfitted with two dozen laptop computers manned by people monitoring election results from each state. Election day turnout models were constantly being updated along with electronic maps detailing turnout in red and blue states. The war room was also outfitted with a bank of television monitors tuned to all the major networks for up-to-date information from around the country. No war room is complete without communication to the outside world, so a number of phones were set up as direct links to key people on the ground in 19 target states across the nation.

As the returns began to come in across the nation, my responsibilities were relegated to making sure management and senior leadership had the requisite amount of Starbucks coffee. Aside from that, it was a thrill to watch 18 months of tireless work come to fruition as the networks began to call state after state for George W. Bush.

With the brief challenge to Ohio by Senator Kerry, we hunkered down for what seemed like hours. At 4:00 a.m. I crawled underneath my cubicle for a few hours of shuteye. I awoke at about 6:30 a.m. and along with the rest of the nation, I waited. Headquarters erupted into cheers a few hours later when it was confirmed that a concession call had taken place. I thought, *Wow. What a great first job out of college.*

Dreams Deferred

As the administration rolled into its fifth year I went to work for communications guru Steve Schmidt. A master of strategic messaging on the campaign, he moved over to the White House to serve as the vice president's top political and communications advisor. It wasn't a sure bet that I'd end up at the White House. To work there is the privilege of such a small minority that I held no illusions of grandeur about the future. The Administration had been going strong for quite some time and there was very little turnover. I served on the inaugural committee, even as I, and many others who worked on the campaign, looked for employment. After going through a number of interviews around Washington D.C., Steve Schmidt took me aside and offered me a position as his executive assistant. I leapt at the opportunity to work for him and serve at the White House, this time as a paid employee.

I worked alongside Schmidt for seven months. As I did so, money became tighter and tighter. All of the staff that worked on the campaign did so for very little money. As an entry-level staffer, it really put a pinch on the bank account. I know I didn't get into government for the money, but all of my student loans were coming due and it was overwhelming. Schmidt went out of his way to help me and there was opportunity to advance and earn a higher wage. The opportunity was to work for Andy Card, the president's chief of staff. I went through three interviews and was encouraged by the prospect.

During the campaign, I was recommended to the chief of staff's office and had interviewed for a separate opportunity that didn't work out. I thought maybe this was a second chance to work for a man whom I deeply admired, but things didn't unfold like I had hoped. When his office went in another direction, I was crushed. I didn't want to leave the White House, knowing deep in my heart how rare it was to work there. The odds of working there again were near impossible, but for financial reasons I made the extremely difficult choice of leaving the very place I had dreamed of working for so many years of my life. In trying to console me Schmidt said, "Everything happens for a reason. Everything will work out." I thanked him for his help and moved on.

It was a dark and difficult time. I could detect no assurance that the future would be bright and that everything would indeed "work out." I'm sure the tug at my heart, "Wait, I will show you something more," was there but in my stubbornness I refused to be encouraged. I slipped up and forgot the advice that had been drilled in my head from boyhood. I didn't take Mom's advice to "put my mind to it," come up with a plan of action and move forward. Her encouragement, "Remember who you are, and who you represent" kept trying to creep up, but I would shove it down in bitterness.

I went to work at a small public affairs firm in Alexandria. Our office overlooked the Potomac and across the river I could see the Capitol to the right and the Washington Monument to the left. I knew that just beyond the Washington Monument was the White House. Thoughts of returning home to Independence dominated my thinking as I scrambled to make sense of how things had turned out. It's apparent now that some of the times in life that bring us the most joy are preceded by the hardest; a confirmation that if something is really worthwhile, it will, more often times than not, require sacrifice, set-backs, discouragement and an abiding faith – that in the end it will be better than all your planning.

I was fortunate to have a few options at home, including furthering my education. In late November 2005, I went to meet with Senator Jim Talent's staff about a position on his campaign back in Kansas City, Missouri. I was impressed by the senator from the moment I met him. He attended the interview, which is rare, and in a very relaxed manner shared his faith, the guiding principles of his life and his vision for leadership. He was a man I could definitely be comfortable working 16-hour-days to re-elect.

On my way home from the Hill I received a call from Rhonda Keenum. Keenum served the president as director of the Public Liaison Office. A superwoman of sorts, she was the mom of triplets. While leading our team she would have another child and return to work within a few days after giving birth. She juggled the enormous responsibilities of White House leadership and tending to her family with effortless ease and grace. She was an atom bomb of energy and creative firepower; a necessary trait for one who led an office responsible for the majority of the events the president participated in around the White House and throughout D.C. When founder of Black Entertainment Television (BET) Bob Johnson created a new bank for the community, it was her idea to have the president visit his new venture and participate in a roundtable on the economy with key stakeholders of the bank.

Schmidt had spoken to her about me previously, but with the difficulty I was having I let fear keep me away. She was reaching out again to see if I would be interested in applying for a position on her staff. She said I'd hear from her in a few days, but then the lines of communication went silent and I began to lose hope once again. I thought that perhaps Keenum had chosen someone else.

Christmas 2005

As December 2005 came to a close, I decided to move back to Missouri and work on Senator Talent's reelection bid. It seemed that nothing was materializing in D.C. and that the run, albeit a good one, was over. I thanked God for the blessing He had given me to serve, even if for a brief time, and for fulfilling one of my dreams. I returned home to Independence for the holidays with scant holiday cheer in my heart. John and Lori Perry recognized I was going through a hard time and graciously invited me on their family vacation to Hawaii. I had never been on a vacation like that before. I was thankful for the opportunity to get away to some warm weather and put off my concerns for the future, even if only for a few days. I found myself on a beach alone on New Year's Day, 2006. After going out and ringing in the New Year alone, I walked along the shoreline. Returning to the hotel at about 1:00 a.m., I was in a pensive state, my mind filled with a tug of war between fear and resolve. The full moon cast a shadowy reflection on the beach and with no city lights to impede their brightness, a million tiny stars shone like points of light against a pitch-black sky. It was a balmy 70 degrees so I decided to stay for a little while and try to ring in the New Year with prayer. I sat down on the beach to begin my vigil. The steady drumbeat of the surf seemed peaceful. I began to reflect on the last six months of financial struggle, walking away from my dream and I tried to ascertain what the future would look like and what I could do to try and help shape it.

Mom's two keys to success surfaced once again from the recesses of my mind. I began to cry to God in my heart for help and for guidance on how to put together a viable plan. I asked for help – any kind of relief to alleviate the current situation of fear and uncertainty. Then my thoughts turned to praise. I suddenly remembered that I was in a tropical paradise on New Year's Day. A billion stars above and a trillion grains of sand beneath and I felt a warmth – not so much by the weather – but a warmth and assurance on the inside that all would turn out OK, and that God had heard my prayer. I thought of the three trees and how this wasn't at all what I had planned – to return home with a dream deferred. But the phrase, "Wait, I will show you something," kindled a feeling of hope. As the steady beat of the waves crashed on the beach in their march to fulfill the measure of their creation, I prayed and hoped for the future. Never had I opened a new year in quite that way – alone, on a beach with a cloudless sky and a symphony of waves. I went back to our hotel room and fell asleep around 3:30 a.m., believing in my heart that all would turn out OK. It did – and it was better than all my planning.

A Welcome Awakening

I was awakened around 5:30 a.m. by the buzzing sound of my cell phone next to my head. As I shook sleep from my eyes and looked at the caller I.D. it registered "202 UNKNOWN." I groaned to myself as I reached for the phone to hit the ignore button and send the "unknown" caller to voicemail before remembering that 202 was the area code for Washington D.C. I hit the button to answer instead and groggily said "Hello."

I was greeted with an energetic and very-much-awake individual on the other end. "Hello, is Lucas there!? This is Jay Zeidman calling on behalf of Rhonda Keenum from the Public Liaison Office at the White House."

My heart skipped a few beats as adrenaline began pumping faster and faster through my veins like I had just received a shot of caffeine. I was suddenly very much awake. "Yes, sir. That's me." I said.

"Great. We need you to come in and fill out some paper work for a background check. And you'll need to take a pee-pee test before you can start work." He said.

Pee-pee test? Who is this guy? I thought.

I stammered, "What? I'm – uh – confused."

Mr. Zeidman continued, "Well you can't start work at the White House without filing paper work for an FBI background check. And we'll need you to take a drug test."

"Wait... am I being offered the position? I hadn't heard back from Mrs. Keenum on the status of the position. I assumed I hadn't been chosen." I said.

Jay replied, "Wow. That's weird. You didn't know? Well that explains why I've had trouble getting a hold of you. We've been trying to reach you for a few days. I mentioned the trouble we were having to your friend, Kevin Curran, in the White House Personnel Office. He gave me your cell phone number so we thought we'd try it before moving on. So pending your initial background check and the results of a drug test, Mrs. Keenum would like you to come back to the White House to work in the Office of Public Liaison as a deputy associate director."

Thank God I didn't eat that poppy seed muffin for breakfast yesterday, I thought to myself. "Wow! This is amazing! Thank you so much. There's just one problem. I'm six hours behind you and I'm in Hawaii for a few more days."

"Ah, I see. No problem. I'll fax the forms to your hotel. If you could fill them out today and fax them back to me I'll start the process. Then when you return to D.C. you can start work."

I learned the salary and offered a silent prayer of praise and thanksgiving. As I hung up the phone, the familiar story read at Christmas a week before caused a shiver. "But God who loves little trees whispered to him, 'Wait. I will show you something.'"

God did show me something more that day. I never thought He would give me a second chance to return to the White House, but He did. And it was better than all my planning.

Back to Service

Friday, January 20, 2006 was a cold and blustery winter day in the nation's capital. But as I waited at the Secret Service checkpoint just inside the entryway to the Eisenhower Executive Office Building (EEOB) I was anything but cold. The EEOB, originally built for the State, War and Navy Departments is an ornate structure built of architecture reminiscent of the second French empire. It actually took 17 years to complete the construction. The EEOB has almost two miles of black and white tiled corridors with eight giant staircases and four skylight domes that double as rotundas. Sitting adjacent to the West Wing, it is a permanent staple of the 18½ acres called the White House complex. The vast majority of the president's staff has office space within the confines of its walls.

Once I was cleared through the system with my date of birth and social security number, I was allowed to proceed up the steps and into the massive building of approximately 550 offices. With a spring in my step and a box of personal items for my desk, I continued up the steep concrete stairs on the north side of the building, facing Pennsylvania Avenue. I exclaimed to myself, *I'm back!* And again whispered a quick prayer of thanks. I was excited at being given another chance to accomplish and fulfill my goal, courtesy of the grace of God and a superwoman named Rhonda Keenum. This time, I resolved not to let go of my dream so easily. I promised myself that I wouldn't let fear of the unknown and the future dominate. It wouldn't be so easy to drive me away this time. Confidence found its place and this time the mission was clear: want to succeed more than you're afraid to fail.

To Everything There Is a Season

The wisdom offered in Ecclesiastes is, "To everything there is a season, and a time to every purpose under the heaven."

Schmidt was right. Everything does happen for a reason. Sometimes to test us, other times to humble us, but at all times to strengthen us. I had gone through a time of breaking down. And while life inevitably has its ebbs and flows, I was convinced at that moment that it was time to build up. Life's seasons, complete with the bitter cold of winter wind and summer's scorching heat, will take their course and make their rounds. Life's full of ups and downs. Some have said it's our decision about how we approach each season and our attitude that determines how we ultimately feel or handle what life puts on the road. Helen Keller, a woman without the ability to hear or see, phrased it best when she said, "Your success and happiness in life lie in you. External conditions are accidents of life. The great enduring realities are love and service. Joy is the holy fire that keeps our purpose warm and our intelligence aglow. Resolve to keep happy, and your joy shall form an invincible host against difficulty."

I stumbled upon a poem by D. H. Groberg during high school, titled *Get Up and Win the Race*. I've carried it with me ever since and pull it out on occasion to remind myself of the importance of never quitting and to keep running – especially when times are tough. Structured like a story, the poem is about a boy who starts out really well in a race, but then trips and falls behind. In an effort to make his father proud and win, he gets up to try again and loses his step to find himself in last place. At one point after the boy had fallen three times he thought about quitting. When he thought about quitting this is what happened next:

Defeat, he lay there silently
A tear dropped from his eye
There's no sense running anymore
Three strikes, I'm out, why try?

The will to rise had disappeared
All hope had fled away
So far behind so error prone
A loser all the way

"I've lost, so what", he thought
I'll live with my disgrace
But then he thought about his dad
Whom soon he'd have to face
"Get up" the echo sounded low
"Get up" and take your place
You were not meant for failure here
"Get up," and win the race

With borrowed will "Get up" it said
"You haven't lost at all"
For winning is no more than this
To rise each time you fall

Sometimes you are ahead. Sometimes you are in the middle of the pack. And sometimes you feel, rightly or not, that you're just dead last. Regardless of where you feel your present condition is, decide within yourself never to quit and to always keep going. The seasons will change but we can always know that if we're willing to "put our mind to it" and act in honor, everything will turn out all right – especially if your drive to succeed is greater than the fear of failure.

CHAPTER NINE

WHITE HOUSE SERVICE

VALUABLE LIFE LESSONS NEVER TO FORGET

*So many of our dreams at first seem impossible,
then they seem improbable, and then, when we
summon the will, they soon become inevitable.*

—Christopher Reeve

Moments to Cherish and Experiences to Remember

It's when the light bulb goes off in your head. It's that moment when your current situation can be viewed with deeper meaning and understanding finds root in your soul. At once, or over time, you're able to harness its impact through positive application for the next few steps in life's journey. That's when you know you've stumbled upon a valuable life lesson. That's when you know it's an enduring principle or experience you should never forget. Serving at the White House wasn't just the fulfillment of a life goal or a dream – it was a training ground for life. A number of key moments impacted me. There were events that molded and stretched me, where

I learned invaluable lessons. Those lessons serve as a guide for how to navigate life's path and respond to the expected and unexpected events that inevitably come our way.

Five years living in Washington D.C. (2003-2008) went by fast, but I always tried to dream big and embrace each moment. Whenever I spoke to a civic or student group that visited the White House, I tried to drive home George Bernard Shaw's words (made famous by Robert Kennedy) "Some men see things as they are and ask why. Others dream things that can be and ask why not."

By watching, doing and making a ton of mistakes with an attitude of "why not" I was fortunate to learn important lessons in leadership, character and how to be successful in personal as well as professional life.

Within a few days of returning to the White House in January 2006, we began planning the president's annual celebration of Black History Month. As weeks and months turned into years, my workload increased and opportunities to take on more responsibilities came my way. I would go on to oversee the president's outreach to the African American community, orchestrating logistics and planning a number of events, including his address to the annual convention of the National Association for the Advancement of Colored People (NAACP). The year 2006 marked the 25th anniversary of the Voting Rights Act. Upon its reauthorization I was fortunate, along with my White House colleague and close friend, Paris Dennard, to plan a large ceremony on the South Lawn. More than 100 members of Congress and over 2,000 community and civic leaders, including stalwarts of the civil rights movement, braved the summer heat of D.C. to celebrate the reauthorization of an act former President Bush said, "Reaffirms we are all created equal." Reverends Jesse Jackson and Al Sharpton came. Civil rights matriarch Dr. Dorothy Height and Dr. King's children

Martin III, Yolanda Denise King and Bernice Albertine King came, too. Former Congressman J.C. Watts was there along with the heads of prominent African American organizations like the NAACP and National Urban League.

Whether it was a big speech, signature event, milestone anniversary or just another day in the office, I soaked up all that I could and always tried to ask myself, *What's the lesson?* As time away from the White House gives way to new chapters and new places in life, I carry with me a few enduring experiences that ultimately became lessons that will always stand out in my mind.

Celebration of Black Music Month 2006 with B.B. King

Monday, June 26, 2006, was supposed to bring more than a thousand people to the South Lawn for an evening celebration of Black Music Month with the country's top jazz and blues performers. After monsoons waterlogged Washington D.C. and the entire Mid Atlantic region the night before and a large elm tree fell on the North Lawn, we settled for a cozy East Room concert instead. The fallen elm tree is featured on the right side of the 20-dollar bill, and it settled close to the front door, partially blocking the path leading up the driveway to the North Portico of the White House. The sun was trying to peek through the clouds as the National Park Service used a number of chain saws to cut up the massive 140-year-old tree for proper removal. I trudged through the puddles up the North Lawn driveway at 1:00 p.m. to meet the performers' representatives for a run through of how the concert would unfold. I noticed just how close the tree had come to actually hitting the White House. *Man, that could have made for a real bad day,* I thought.

The Gulf Coast region (Louisiana and Mississippi) is known for its amazing musical contributions. New Orleans, specifically, is known as the birthplace of jazz. In light of what had occurred a little less than a year before with Hurricane Katrina, Rhonda Keenum gave me and my deputy, Paris Dennard, direction on the theme for that year, and even secured our main act months in advance. She called me into her office and gave me the numbers for B.B. King's managers in New York and Los Angeles. We were going to celebrate the Gulf Coast with a tribute to blues, jazz, and soul.

There is a commonly known acronym that Secret Service and White House staff use to refer to the president and other senior administration officials. The president is POTUS, short for President of the United States. The first lady is referred to as FLOTUS, or First Lady of the United States. I received a nickname from my colleagues, as a joke, along similar lines. Somehow the nickname stuck and Paris and I were referred to as BLOTUS and DBLOTUS. It was short for Black Liaison of the United States and Deputy Black Liaison of the United States. When I was promoted to other responsibilities, Paris took on the title BLOTUS and dubbed me BLOTUS Emeritus.

After Keenum secured the main event, Paris and I went to work sketching out the rest of the concert. We decided to kick off the celebration with the Cultural Ambassador of New Orleans Irvin Mayfield, follow him up with a little scat from legendary soul performer Patti Austin and have a grand finale with the King of the Blues.

Trumpeter Irvin Mayfield was only 28 years old and performing on stage in the East Room. The moment was a big one, not so much for the 225 guests all crammed into the East Room, or the cadre of national press, but for Irvin. He had endured a great deal of heartache that led him to that place and time – to perform for the president. He performed *Just a Closer Walk with Thee*, a song of special and personal

> *The blues is really the story of true American optimism; that when things are going wrong you can always be all right.*
>
> **—Irvin Mayfield**

significance. Irvin performed in numerous Hurricane Katrina relief fundraisers during a time of great adversity. We learned his father, Irvin Mayfield, Sr., was identified as a victim of Hurricane Katrina on November 20, 2005. Irvin went three months without knowing his father's whereabouts before receiving the fateful news. He performed the tune the same way it would be played for a traditional funeral procession in New Orleans. The procession moves gradually through the streets, followed by a band playing a sad song. The custom is that once the casket has been laid in place, the group breaks into an upbeat second line, symbolizing the "Triumph of the spirit over death."

Just a Closer Walk with Thee was the first song Irvin learned from his late father. He played it in honor of his dad after the hurricane and then retired the song. He brought it out of retirement to play one last time for the president in celebration of Black Music Month.

Before his performance, Irvin spoke about what jazz and the blues meant to him before a White House audience rapt with attention. He said, "Jazz is the manifestation of democracy in music."

As he spoke about his dad and the honor of retiring the song in his memory in front of the president, he reminded us that music is often the key to go from mourning to dancing.

"The blues," he said "is really the story of true American optimism; that when things are going wrong you can always be all right."

He encouraged us to get past obstacles and heartache, overcome our mourning and pass onto celebration.

The notes from his trumpet echoed through the East Room and beyond the open doorway through the Cross Hall and into the State Dining Room. In the shadow of an original full length Gilbert Stuart portrait of George Washington, the sound that came from Irvin's trumpet filled the audience with awe. As he reached the joyful second line, with our undivided attention, Irvin did his father proud, and in one accord the entire crowd rose to their feet to give him a rousing standing ovation. I'm sure his father was smiling down on him and cheering his son along with us.

The legendary Patti Austin sang *How High the Moon* and *How Do You Keep the Music Playing*. The goddaughter of Quincy Jones, we learned that Patti Austin had performed for every president since Ronald Reagan. President Bush said this about Patti, before her performance, "When she was rehearsing her performance for President Reagan, Patti was singing so powerfully a piece of molding fell from the ceiling here in the East Room. Be forewarned," he deadpanned, "when Patti sings, she brings down the house."

Patti did just that on that soggy, rain soaked summer day.

An ornate red carpet extends through the Cross Hall connecting the East Room and the State Dining Room. If you've ever seen a president hold a press conference in the East Room, you've seen him take a confident long walk down the red carpet as the announcement is made, *Ladies and Gentlemen, the President of the United States.*

B.B. King grew up a sharecropper with an eighth-grade education and there he was, almost 81 at the time, still going strong and performing for a United States president. An amiable, jolly man possessed with a gift of incredible charm and wit, the only special request he had was that we have a chair for him on stage. I marveled at his humility.

During rehearsal the band decided the equipment we rented from the local music store didn't allow them to play as loud as they wanted. They were about to retrieve their mega amplifiers from the tour bus to liven things up a bit when Paris alerted me to the problem. I got a little nervous at the request. As the largest room in the house, the East Room is just shy of 80 by 37 feet. The ceiling serves as an anchor to three massive bohemian cut chandeliers purchased in 1902 during former President Teddy Roosevelt's White House renovation. With them weighing around a thousand pounds each and being so old I didn't want to be the guy responsible when they fell from the ceiling thanks to the bass vibration of the blues. We brokered a compromise. B.B. and the band could play with as much gusto as they liked, but we would use the amplifiers and equipment we had rented for their use from the local music store just in case. Our equipment wasn't as advanced as theirs, but then again the White House is over 200 years old.

The Cross Hall, connecting the East Room with other rooms on the second floor of the residence, is lighted by two Adam-style cut-glass chandeliers made in London around 1775. I stood just outside the doorway of the Cross Hall with Paris to watch B.B. and his band perform; to my right and left – portraits of former presidents looked on in stately repose. Seated in the front row was President Bush and next to him was Basketball Hall of Famer Kareem Abdul Jabbar.

Mom had never been to the White House before and it was her first time ever to attend an event. She was as excited about hearing the President speak as she was meeting Kareem Abdul Jabbar. Never mind that Mom and Dad were probably two of five white people in the entire audience; they felt completely at home, which was made possible because we were in the presence of the King of the Blues. B.B. performed *Why I Sing the Blues, I Need You So, When Love Comes to Town,* and of course... *The Thrill Is Gone.*

During B.B.'s last song, the president's personal aide, Jared Weinstein, came up behind me and whispered, "Did you ever think a small town kid from Independence, Missouri would be here watching B.B. King play for the president with his mom in the audience?"

With all the planning, scurrying around and responsibilities for ensuring the concert went off without a hitch, the true significance of the moment had almost passed me by. I looked back at Jared as the significance of the moment fully set in.

"Wow, no, I didn't." I replied.

He gave me a pat on the shoulder. "Take it in."

I was standing in the famous Cross Hall of the White House and the King of Blues was strumming his guitar.

After the concert was over, I escorted B.B. King and his band back to their tour bus and we began to share our life stories with each other. B.B. told me what an honor it was for him to perform and I thanked him for a fantastic performance. I mentioned his humble beginnings and what an inspiration his unique story of coming up from nothing was for those in attendance. He was as humble as can be and asked me about my story and how I got to the White House. I shared with him my beginnings while holding an umbrella over him to protect him from the rain. He gave me a big hug, looked me straight in the eye, and said, "I'm proud to be a black man walking with you out of the White House today. I'm proud of you."

The King of the Blues said he was proud of me. It's a moment I'll never forget.

Dr. Martin Luther King Junior Groundbreaking

November 13, 2006, was a brisk and cold, but nonetheless, historic Monday in the nation's capital. A few days after the midterm elections and just a few blocks from the White House near the Tidal Basin between the Lincoln and Jefferson Memorials, there would be a new memorial dedicated to the legacy of Dr. Martin Luther King Jr. Any monument is historic, but this one was especially so, in that it was to be the first monument to a black American on the National Mall. The drizzle of rain from an overcast sky couldn't deter thousands of people from descending on the National Mall and breaking ground. Dr. King's children, Martin Luther King III, Yolanda Denise King and Bernice Albertine King, gathered on stage with celebrities like Oprah Winfrey and Tommy Hilfiger. Members of Congress and VIPs of presidential administrations past and present were in attendance. Secretary of State Condoleezza Rice joined President Bush for the short three-minute motorcade from the White House to the National Mall. Former President Clinton gave remarks as well. A future president was on stage that day, too. If the crowd knew then what we all know now, perhaps they would have taken more note of his remarks and a lot more photographs. Then-Senator Barack Obama said:

> *Through words he [MLK] gave voice to the voiceless. Through deeds he gave courage to the faint of heart. By dint of vision, and determination, and most of all faith in the redeeming power of love, he endured the humiliation of arrest, the loneliness of a prison cell, the constant threats to his life, until he finally inspired a nation to transform itself, and begin to live up to the meaning of its creed.*

> *Like Moses before him, he would never live to see the Promised Land. But from the mountain top, he pointed the way for us— a land no longer torn asunder with racial hatred and ethnic strife, a land that measured itself by how it treats the least of*

these, a land in which strength is defined not simply by the
capacity to wage war but by the determination to forge peace –
a land in which all of God's children might come together in a
spirit of brotherhood.

I didn't fully grasp the meaning of his words until weeks later. As I replayed the event in my mind, an unfamiliar scene unfolded. After President Bush's remarks I saw him and former President Clinton in a huddle backstage with Senior Advisor Karl Rove and Oprah Winfrey. They were having a hearty, amiable discussion about MLK and the outcome of the midterm elections a week prior. While political opposites and opponents on the field of politics, they were united in one cause on that rainy field off the Potomac River that day. Just a few days removed from an election and decades after his assassination, Dr. King was still bringing us, Democrats and Republicans, together.

As luminaries lined up to place their shovels in the mud I witnessed one of the most courageous individuals of the civil rights era, Congressman John Lewis of Georgia, break down in tears as the profundity of the moment overwhelmed him. Joined with Reverend Jesse Jackson and Ambassador Andrew Young, they seemed like brothers in arms at the end of a long, hard war. They held each other up, reflected on the civil rights battles of the past and celebrated with reverence the monument to come.

Tuskegee Airmen Congressional Gold Medal Ceremony

The Congressional Gold Medal is the highest civilian award the United States Congress bestows. Many have received it, but on Thursday, March 29, 2007, the ceremony that took place in the Capitol Hill Rotunda for more than 300 veterans was an especially memorable moment in our nation's history. Hundreds of people had come from every corner of the country to cram themselves beneath the large dome to pay tribute to the Tuskegee Airmen. As the old Negro spiritual says, "It had been a long time comin'."

The airmen were African American pilots who flew with distinction during World War II. Prior to their service, no African Americans had ever served in the military as pilots. The old veterans were a delight. The vast majority of them were over the age of 75 and in wheel chairs. Some were in plain dark suits while others wore bright red or powder blue blazers decked with medals, commendations and testaments to their service.

Before the actual ceremony, the president and Speaker Pelosi took a photo with the airmen in Statuary Hall. Trying to coral 300 plus Tuskegee Airmen, most in wheel chairs, was no easy task. In fact – it was chaos. Trying to line up 200 wheel chairs in a semicircle, followed by those who could walk, was a harder task than it first seemed.

"Stagecoach," the Secret Service code name for the president's motorcade, was about five minutes out and I still hadn't accomplished anything close to resembling a good lineup for a photo in Statuary Hall. Some kept wandering off looking at the statues. Others were chatting excitedly with their family and friends who kept trying to be in the picture. A White House photographer had come ahead of the entourage to help me arrange the veterans in proper order. I had them lined up – kind of – and then we had to turn them all around to face the other direction. Comedy at its finest!

An astute observer had noticed one of the statues that would be in the background of the photo was of a Southern general of the Confederacy. That could be construed as offensive. So we did an about-face and tried the line up from another angle.

Advance Trip Director Jason Recher radioed from the motorcade. He needed a status report. Recher was the guy who regularly briefed the president on logistics, movements and next steps when the president left the White House and traveled abroad. Recher spoke into the mouthpiece attached to the communication radio on his belt, "Are the airmen and Speaker Pelosi ready for arrival and group photo?"

"Uh, not quite," I responded. "We are almost there."

"What seems to be the problem?" asked Recher.

Not really wanting to tell him that the "animals had left the zoo and I couldn't get them back in their cage," I opted for the non-answer-answer. "Give me five minutes and we should be all set."

What I really needed was another 30 minutes to situate the Tuskegee Airmen into a coherent formation. I didn't want to tell Recher and the other 30 or so people who were listening on the secure radio channel that we ran into a little snafu and had to turn them all around. It didn't matter though. The airmen were happy to oblige and so excited. I couldn't blame them. Heck, I was proud of them. This was their moment.

Once the president arrived he and Speaker Pelosi proceeded to Statuary Hall for the photo. If you've ever seen an artist take a big paint brush, dip it in a bunch of different buckets of paint and then throw it on the canvas with abandon, that's what the room looked like.

Recher looked at me and said, "Are you kidding me? Is this a joke?"

I sheepishly replied, "Bro, it's been a day."

While different in their outer appearance and varying in age, the airmen all shared a common bond and a sense of overwhelming pride in what they had accomplished in service to their country. The lesson these men taught me was powerful. Their example was one of constant sacrifice. They willingly served their country and for most of them, their country didn't return the favor. In some instances they were never given a proper salute. They suffered indignity, humiliation, went without deserved promotions and persevered through extreme prejudice. The president's remarks reflected the hardship they went through, "Their every mission, their every success, their every failure viewed through the color of their skin. Yet they were proud of their country even though their country wasn't proud of them."

I tried to shake as many of the heroes' hands as possible. I was hoping that in being near them I could glean some wisdom. I grew up not knowing or ever meeting my birth father. I wonder to this day what he looked like, who he was, where he is and whether he is alive. The only black role models I had growing up were in books. Mom had me read the story of Jackie Robinson and how he broke the color barrier in baseball. She also had me read the story of Dr. Ben Carson, the famous neurosurgeon at Johns Hopkins Hospital, who was awarded the Presidential Medal of Freedom in 2008. Growing up, he had difficulty in school, just like me, and went through his share of adversity. His mom, like mine, began to instill in him the value of being built for something more. Countless impacted and saved lives are thankful Ben Carson believed his mother and decided to take another path in life.

For a fleeting moment, spending time with the Tuskegee Airmen served to fill a void I didn't know I had. Statuary Hall is filled with statues of heroes from across the nation; but those are heroes whose hearts have stopped beating. All in attendance at the ceremony had the distinct honor of being in the presence of real heroes who were very much alive. House Speaker Nancy Pelosi, Senate Majority Leader Harry Reid and former Secretary of State Collin Powell all offered their tributes. As former President Bush spoke, his words traveled to each heart in the room.

The speaker and I had the honor of having our picture taken with you, and as I walked into the rotunda I was impressed by the fact that I wasn't amongst heroes who were statues. I was impressed that I was amongst heroes who still live.

I stood back stage watching the ceremony on a television monitor with Jason Recher and the president's aide, Jared Weinstein, as Bush continued,

The Tuskegee Airmen helped win a war, and helped change our nation for the better. Yours is the story of the human spirit, and it ends like all great stories do — with wisdom and lessons and hope for tomorrow. And the medal that we confer today means that we're doing a small part to ensure that your story will be told and honored for generations to come.

As the president ended his remarks he did and said something remarkable — and the scene is etched into my memory to this day.

I would like to offer a gesture to help atone for all the unre-turned salutes and unforgivable indignities. And so, on behalf of the office I hold, and a country that honors you, I salute you for your service to the United States of America.

As the president raised his right hand and offered a crisp salute, his face etched with tears, the seated soldiers leapt to their feet as fast as humanly possible to reciprocate the gesture. It didn't matter whether they had canes or were in wheelchairs, they stood as they were able. They rose from their chairs and returned their commander in chief's salute.

The Second Anniversary of Hurricane Katrina

Dr. Doris Hicks was incredulous. Standing at 5 feet, 10 inches with a thick Cajun accent, she was a woman who exuded absolute confidence and control. She reminded me of movie producer Tyler Perry's famous character Madea Simmons, except that Madea had gray hair. There was no growing old for this super hero! The day I met her she was sharply dressed in a crisp, black pants suit, with a fresh perm of giant red curls. Students and teachers from pre-k through ninth grade respected Dr. Hicks for leading them through a time of great adversity. The school – teachers, parents, and students alike –were her family. Her mission was to spur them on and encourage them to rise from beneath the floodwaters that overtook them. Dr Hick's school, located in the Lower Ninth Ward of New Orleans, was engulfed with water reaching past the second floor when Katrina breached the levees on August 29th 2005.

The matriarch of *Dr. Martin Luther King Jr. Charter School for Math and Science* is another one of those unsung heroes I've mentioned. She might have been unnoticed by the rest of us, but those in the Lower Ninth Ward knew of her courage and leadership well. While no one was present at the school during the storm, some of her students didn't make it through. Hers was the arduous task of building anew while holding a young and impressionable student body together amidst unspeakable grief.

She was a mother and healer; there to comfort and unite. She was the rebuilder. And that wasn't even her day job. Beyond that, she had to ensure the children didn't miss a beat and continued to receive an exceptional education.

As the second anniversary of Hurricane Katrina neared, we planned for the president to visit her school, hold a round table on education, and share with her and her students in a moment of silence at 9:38 a.m., the precise moment the levees broke.

"Y'all wanna have *who* come here?" She exclaimed, "I don't believe it."

The White House point man for the trip, Jason Recher, and I were in her office to inquire if she would be interested in a visit from the president of the United States. Jason gave me a sideways glance. We didn't quite know how this meeting would pan out. Would she throw us out and curse the president in the process? It had been two years and we were very sensitive to the raw emotion this anniversary might evoke. It wasn't our intent to inflame passions or conjure up old wounds and sadness. We wanted to tread lightly and not in any way press her to host. We had decided if she wasn't amenable to a visit that we would graciously be on our way and plan some other activities for the commemoration. Recher poured on some good old gentlemanly Southern charm.

"Yes ma'am, it was originally planned to have the secretary of education visit but if you wouldn't mind, President and Mrs. Bush would like to take a brief tour of your renovated school, visit with your students and share in a moment of silence," Recher told her.

"You gotta be kiddin me!" she exclaimed. "Wow! The president wants to come here!? I can't tell you how much I love Mrs. Bush."

A smile crept across my face. A woman of consummate grace and an easy-going nature, the former first lady evoked calm and good feelings anywhere she went. She was above the fray of politics and her approval rating showed it.

"No ma'am. We aren't trying to pull your leg." Recher replied.

I wish we had brought a Staples "That was easy" button, but Recher finally convinced her we really worked for the White House and the president really did want to visit her school.

Moment of Silence

The morning of August 29, 2007 began very early for the Secret Service. Nationally syndicated radio host Tom Joyner was broadcasting from the cafeteria to drive awareness for the anniversary. Among his guests were the Reverend Al Sharpton and New Orleans Mayor Ray Nagin. Set to go on air at 5:00 a.m., bomb-sniffing dogs with Secret Service in tow began their security sweep of the building two hours earlier. As the event contact, I had to be on-site to manage the hundreds of guests who had to be patted down and go through the metal detectors in advance of the first couple's visit later that morning.

As the time for the president's arrival drew near, the children's energy level kicked up a few notches. We stationed the majority of them in the cafeteria, the site of the radio show earlier, and the rest in classrooms Mr. and Mrs. Bush would stop in during their visit. The children in the cafeteria watched the moment of silence on closed circuit television. At about 9:36, President and Mrs. Bush walked into the library with Dr. Doris Hicks and a half dozen students at their side. The small school library was packed. We had moved a number of shelves to make room for the guests, but it seemed there still wasn't enough space. Former Governor Kathleen Blanco and former Congressman William Jefferson joined with about 50 community leaders, students, teachers and the national press to bow their heads in remembrance at the appointed time. A few moments before the hour Dr. Hicks took to the podium and introduced the president. With optimism and just the right touch of grace, Principal Hicks offered a nod of respect to the past, and looked with faith towards a brighter day. As she concluded her remarks, I thought to myself, *another hero for the silent witness of history.*

Equipped with a set of drums, and a few brass instruments, the school band belted out a simple, but effective, rendition of *Hail to the Chief* as Mr. and Mrs. Bush entered the cafeteria a few minutes later. The rest of the students, decked out in their uniforms of black slacks, white blouses and red and green skirts, gave a hearty yelp in unison with the band. They had practiced diligently for the visit; it was supposed to be a surprise. And surprise the president they did.

The motorcade, an impressive fleet of about 20 vehicles, including a number of white multi-passenger vans, black Chevrolet Suburbans, a few sedans and an ambulance, began to roll towards its next destination on the president's schedule. Traffic stopped as the roads were cleared by local law enforcement. Dr. Hicks stood at my side as Mr. and Mrs. Bush waved goodbye from behind the bullet-proof glass window of their black armored Suburban.

"How'd our little school do?" she asked once the last van finally passed.

If she only knew.

Dr. Hicks and her students showed me what optimism through the storms of life really mean. I was only with her bright-eyed students for a few days, but their example of perseverance and optimistic perspective stays with me.

A Dream Come True: Air Force One

That wasn't the only thing about the second anniversary of Hurricane Katrina that was memorable. Jason pulled me aside the day before the president's arrival in New Orleans to give me a piece of unexpected news. Typically, when we worked on events outside of Washington D.C., the White House would fly us via commercial airliner to the designated city. I fully expected to fly back to D.C. the same way I had flown to New Orleans, in coach. Recher said that while the plane would almost certainly be at capacity, he was working to get me a seat on Air Force One for the trip back to the nation's capital. I didn't believe it at first. It came out of left field and was so unexpected. Deputy Director of Advance John Meyer gave up his seat so I could have the opportunity. When Recher delivered the news I tried to contain myself, but it was too much. I wanted to jump up and down like I'd just won a million-dollar jackpot in Las Vegas.

The plan was to say my goodbyes to Dr. Hicks, the teachers and students and hightail it to the landing zone to await helicopter lift. The president was scheduled to attend an event and deliver remarks in southern Mississippi in commemoration of the anniversary. Recher and I weren't involved in the planning of those stops so we would transport by helicopter with the rest of the president's traveling staff to a landing zone in Mississippi. After unloading, the plan was to fly by helicopter to the awaiting presidential plane and hold until the rest of the schedule was complete.

I had about 30 minutes to get to the landing zone in time to depart with the rest of the traveling staff. I estimated it would be about a 15-minute drive, leaving a 15-minute cushion. I pulled out of the school's parking lot in my rented sedan, drove to the light to turn right and cross the Judge Seeber Bridge when I suddenly came upon bumper-to-bumper traffic. *Oh No! Traffic is still backed up from the president's motorcade. I'll never make it*, I thought. I crawled along for about five minutes, gripping the steering wheel tighter and tighter as each wasted moment passed by. My dream flashed before my eyes. I saw the movie *Air Force One* when it came out in the theaters in 1997. Here was my chance. A fellow White House staffer had even given up his own seat and the moment was about to pass me by. I offered a quick prayer to God for help. As I inched up towards the next intersection I waved down the police officer holding traffic.

"Is traffic still backed up from the president?" I asked.

"No," he replied. "There is a parade proceeding across the bridge into the Lower Ninth Ward to commemorate the anniversary."

"Oh, I see. Well, look sir. I have a real problem. I'm with the president's staff."

At first, he gave me this look that said, "Sure you are." I showed him my White House badge and told him I could have him call the school to confirm I was part of the president's staff that assisted with the event.

"Why aren't you with the president now if you work for him?" He challenged.

I was losing my patience. "Sir, he has other events in town today and is due at the landing zone in a few minutes. If I don't make it I'll be left."

I was able to convince him I was legitimate.

"OK. Let me see what I can do," he relented.

The officer walked over to another officer for a chat and pointed back in my direction.

As the officer came back over I thought to myself *God, I hope this works. If not, I'm toast. Just stay calm Lucas. Everything will work out. Just stay calm. You'll make it… somehow.*

"Ok. I got approval to escort you across the bridge," the officer said.

Whew! A sigh of relief escaped my lips. "Thank you, sir. I really appreciate your help," I offered.

"No problem," he replied. "Follow close behind. The lane going your direction is open. We just need to get you past this traffic."

I did as the officer directed and thanked him once again. Once I crossed over the Industrial Canal and was out of sight of the police I turned right and punched the accelerator. When I arrived at the landing zone I asked the Secret Service what the president's arrival time was estimated to be. We had a few more minutes than I thought. The president, uncharacteristically, was running behind. Boy, was I was glad he was running late that day.

Tour of a Lifetime

The Night Hawk helicopter touched down on the tarmac. Once the Army pilot shut down the engines and the rotors ceased to spin, I walked down the ramp towards the back door and proceeded to disembark from the helicopter. There she was. Set against a gorgeous backdrop of large cumulus clouds and a crystal clear blue sky, Special Air Mission 2800, known as Air Force One when the president was onboard, stood majestic. It felt like Christmas morning as I walked towards the fulfillment of a dream. I took in a deep breath and exhaled. I could hardly contain how excited I was. I took out my camera and began snapping pictures. Recher and the rest of the staff looked back at me wondering if I was gonna keep up. They were all old hands at this stuff. I wanted to pinch myself. *Is this real?* I thought. After taking a few photos I walked up through the ground floor entry of Air Force One and took the steps up to the second level. I was aboard one of the most visible and recognizable symbols of the presidency of the United States. Like a kid in Willy Wonka's chocolate factory, I was on sensory overload.

Since Air Force One was holding until the president finished his event in Mississippi we had about an hour till departure. Recher arranged with one of the Air Force personnel for a tour of the plane. The airmen not only took care of the needs of president, staff, Secret Service, guests and press, but were also active duty military personnel. Being "stationed" on Air Force One was one of the highest honors for active duty Air Force personnel. In my excitement I peppered my patient guide with a volley of questions about the plane. He took me to see the president's office. As he told me about the room and what sorts of things took place there, I thought of 9/11 and the pictures we had all seen of the president at this desk peering out the window talking on the phone with the vice president. That day the plane had served as a command center and epicenter for managing the crisis. A dark navy blue jacket hung over the back of the president's chair. The seal of the president and the words President George W. Bush were emblazoned on the right breast. My guide took me up to the cockpit to meet the pilots and communications crew that kept the giant bird in the air. I looked out the window from the cockpit and learned we were about three stories up. I shook my head in disbelief. As I looked over all the state-of-the-art equipment I couldn't really make sense of it, I quipped that it didn't quite look like the plane in the movie. I got a slight smile in return. He was probably thinking, *If I had a buck for every time I heard that one.*

"No. The president doesn't have an escape pod," he smiled in reply.

The Air Force steward explained to me what the custom-made version of a normal Boeing 747 did have, though. With more than 4,000 feet of interior floor space, a conference room, medical facility, two kitchens, state-of-the-art navigation systems, the whole place seemed to me like a posh house or executive suite office space in the air. My guide went on to explain that the plane was capable of refueling midair and its communications are configured to withstand any foreign attack. The advanced secure communications equipment can basically turn the plane into a flying bunker. The tour was amazing. It was better than any book I had read on the plane. *Wait, I will show you something,* echoed in my mind. It was better than all my planning.

When the president, Mrs. Bush and the rest of the staff arrived, I found out that my mentor, then Secretary of Housing and Urban Development Alphonso Jackson would be flying with us. I took a piece of Air Force One stationery over to him and asked him to sign it as a keepsake, and he obliged. I'll always remember his words of encouragement and advice to me when I went to meet with him as a young intern five years prior:

Lucas, always remember, if you can look up you can get up.

I've reminded myself of his advice several times since. Anytime I'm feeling like I don't have enough in the tank to get to the next gas station to refuel, his words are among the things that I use to keep me going.

Phone Call to Mom from Air Force One

As I buckled my seat belt in the guest cabin for the flight to D.C., Recher came back to check on me. He said I could make a call if I wanted to. There was only one person in the world I could think of to call ... my hero. I picked up the secure white telephone installed into the railing along the window. Instead of a dial tone, one of the communications attendants I had seen earlier on my tour came on the line. Apparently, you don't make your own phone calls on Air Force One. Who knew?! The Air Force personnel communicate with the intended recipient on your behalf with a call sign of Air Force One. Once they have the intended recipient on the line, they patch the call through. With a plane that can hold up to 70 passengers, you can imagine how busy a crew of 26 is during a cross-country flight. The duties Air Force personnel have to perform on any given flight are staggering – preparing and serving food, flying the plane, taking care of other essential needs, and providing support to staff, allowing us to continue working as if we were at our desks back at the White House.

I explained to the Air Force crewmember who I was, that it was my first flight, and that I wanted to surprise my mom with a call. Mom had no idea that any of this was even happening that day. He asked for her name and the number to reach her. He said he would call me back when he had connected. I hung up the phone and anxiously awaited his return call. The phone rang and I pulled it out of its cradle. The crewmember relayed that no one was answering at the home number. A little crestfallen, I racked my brain to try and remember Mom's work number at the local library in Independence. I retrieved it from my cell phone and snatched the phone from its cradle to try once more.

After a few minutes the operator came back on the line and said, "Lucas, I have your mom for you. Here she is."

"Mom, are you there?" I asked.

She replied with some hesitation at first, "Lucas…Are you OK? Is this … real?"

"Yes Mom. It's me. I'm on Air Force One and I wanted to call you!"

There was silence on the other end for a few moments. Then the distinct sound of sniffles as my mom began to cry. "Oh Lucas, what a wonderful blessing."

As she began to cry I found myself choked up as well. She, more than anyone, knew what it meant for me to be able to fly on Air Force One. To be able to express my gratitude to her on the phone at 35,000 feet onboard one of the world's most famous aircrafts was overwhelming. I told her briefly how excited – actually giddy – I was and thanked her for a life of love and constant prodding to map out a plan to go and "put my mind to it."

Mom remembers almost everything about that day, August 29, 2007. It was a scorcher in Missouri and with library work often requiring some physical labor, Mom made it a point to be as comfortable as the humid August weather would let her. She opted for a black t-shirt, light cotton skirt, and comfortable sandals. I've found that women are always so good at remembering neat things like what they were wearing when an important event occurs in their life! I always laugh when Mom relates how the event unfolded from her side of the phone.

Almost all families with working mothers have a rule for getting a hold of Mom while she's at work. In our family we adhere to the "Don't call unless there is blood or you can't breathe" rule. So, I was just a bit perplexed when, going out of the workroom to take my turn on the desk at the library, my colleague Marge looked up and told me that there had been a phone call for me but no one knew where I was and so the caller had said that he'd call back in a few minutes. Peevishly I squabbled to myself, "They know the rule." Soon someone said that there was a phone call for me, and Marge said, "That must be him. He sounded serious and 'official' Dot."

I have such an uneventful life, it didn't occur to me that anything untoward could have happened to anyone in my family, but I remember that Marge hung around. In retrospect, I'm sure she was concerned about the content of the call and wanted to be close "just in case." For my part, I was more than oblivious when I answered, "This is Dot; how may I help you?" "Dorothy Boyce?" Well, my. Did I say "official"? To the point of being comical or stereotypical, this was a serious voice talking to me; deep, even-toned, a la Gary Owens from the old "Laugh In" program. As a matter of fact, that's exactly the picture that popped into my head. I could just "see" this voice with his left hand cupped around his ear as he spoke! "Yes?" "Please hold for a call from Air Force One," said the serious sounding voice. "Right. Sure. You're putting me on, right?" By now I was sure my fellow workers were back in the workroom, giggling their collective heads off as their latest prank on how to get ol' Dot unfolded. I could imagine their plan to repeat the story to everyone in the library! The response from the voice on the other end dashed that thought to pieces. "No ma'am, I am not. Please hold," concluded Mr. Serious Official, Gary Owens wanna be. And with that, the cheerful voice of my son came on the line, "Hello? Mom?"

Since he was very young, Lucas had these dreams or goals he kept sharing with us. One was working at the White House, a dream realized when he earned the privilege of serving former President George W. Bush. The second was flying aboard Air Force One, a dream being fulfilled in real time, with me on the phone with him. It was honestly too big a moment to even know what to say. There were almost no words. My face turned beet red and my eyes filled with tears.

Almost always, when there is a big event in the life of Lucas, my first thoughts are to his gene pool, to the people who went before him and made, not just this life possible for him, but imbued him with certain possibilities, that, uncovered, would one day lead to the full, complete Lucas. So, as always, my first thoughts went to sights unseen by me, then to sights seen: Sweeping up hair at the beauty shop at the age of 17 months, putting on my apron and vacuuming with serious intent at the age of three, and playing "dress-ups" in every kind of garb imaginable all through his early life. Once, watching him run up and down the hill in our backyard, wearing a bucket on his head while pretending to be a fireman, Aunt Donnie said, "My word you don't dare let him watch "The King and I," he'd go off and shave his head! My thoughts turned to the summer he worked so hard at a two-week dance clinic, coming home and laying on the floor, crying, exhausted, but eager to go back the next day and later declaring it the best two weeks of his activity-filled summer. Maybe once in ten years I had to remind him to practice his piano lesson. Yes, I said once, and I'll bet Lucas would say that was an exaggeration, as I probably never had to remind him, but did once just to see how it felt! I recalled how during his teenage years, when his favorite pastime, like most teens, seemed to be scoffing at Mom, I had to put my sensitive self aside for a while and "stick to my guns."

But as I stood there with the phone in my hand the same as any other mother, realizing this rare moment, I didn't want this particular moment in our life to end. I wanted, for once, to be clever, to say the "right" memorable thing. Mostly I think I just giggled and cried, but standing there, looking at the clock in the workroom ticking off the minutes, elated as I was, I was still aware that I was at work! I also flashed back to my ninth grade speech class and a quote [from English biologist Thomas Henry Huxley] on which I had to give a speech: "The rung of a ladder is not meant to rest upon, but only to hold a man's foot long enough to enable him to put the other somewhat higher," and I knew that this was Lucas' present rung and it was so very, very enjoyable to be there and humbling to realize that he was trying, as best he could, to have us be there together.

CHAPTER TEN

THE NATIVE SON RETURNS HOME

Where I was conceived
And where I first believed
With a heart full of goals and longings to soar
where I was taught I could fly, where I dreamed I could do more

My spring-board and my expected end
Home base for family, for mentors, and friends
And when it's just me in the midst of this
race called life – and I am alone?
My thoughts will always turn to mom, to Independence, to home

There is nothing half so pleasant, as coming home again
—Margaret Elizabeth Sangster
The Date: January 31, 2008
Thursday Evening
Aboard Air Force One

I had flown home to Kansas City International Airport several times in the five years I lived in Washington D.C. There were the typical reasons – a friend or family member's wedding, holiday gatherings, or to volunteer at a youth camp. This time was different.

Two days after his last State of the Union Address before a joint session of the 110th Congress, I, along with the usual suspects of senior and junior White House staff, Secret Service, military personnel, and the national press corps found ourselves on a cross-country jaunt to promote the president's agenda as he entered the twilight of his presidency. I didn't realize it when we left Andrews Air Force Base three days prior, but the last stop of the trip proved to be one of the most memorable and exhilarating 12 hours of the first 28 years of my life. At approximately 8:00 p.m. MST, as we flew at about 35, 000 feet over the Rocky Mountains, toward Kansas City International Airport, it hit me, *I'm going home.* A three-day swing through four states and a series of 12 events including a tour and remarks at a helicopter company, a speech on the global war on terror, a bill signing proclaiming February as Healthy Heart Month, a breakfast with small business leaders and entrepreneurs on the economy, and a political fundraiser for our hometown Congressman Sam Graves.

It was my first extended trip with the president. Planning and executing these events, along with a team of White House aides, was an incredible responsibility and honor to be entrusted with. Nothing happened without teamwork in our world so I was thankful to have a lot of help. Whether it was staff from communications, speech writing, the military office, the Air Force, advance staff, the press office, or the Secret Service, everyone pitched in to make each event unique and exceptional.

We had just finished a political event in Cherry Hills, Colorado for a U.S. Senate candidate and were aboard Air Force One en route to Missouri, the last state on the itinerary as the sun went down. This time flying home was different for the very fact that I wouldn't be taxiing to the main terminal and waiting for my luggage at the nearest baggage claim. Typically, I'd book a flight on Southwest Airlines, Midwest Express, Air Tran or United. On that crisp winter night the United States Air Force trumped them all. It's difficult to describe the simple boyish thrill that went through me to be able to fulfill the life-long dream of flying aboard that plane. I'd only had the privilege to fly one other time since the Hurricane Katrina trip a year prior. I was ever cognizant of the privilege and honor to fly aboard Air Force One; and beyond humbled by the grace that made it possible. It was never a given that you would travel with the president. Resolved that I would never take it for granted, the same feelings of awe and honor I felt the first time remained.

Did I Just Sit in Your Chair Mr. President?

As we careened across the sky en route to Kansas City, I needed to brief the president's senior advisor, Barry Jackson, on the next days' events. I walked towards the conference room where I knew he and the other high-ranking staff would be. A number of senior aides were present. The room doubled as a dining room for the president, but also functioned as "office space" for senior staff. Most of the seats were taken so I sat down next to Barry Jackson – the nearest available seat to him. I didn't think anything was wrong with it at the time, but it was at the head of the table – which meant it was the president's seat. This of course didn't dawn on me – until the president walked in and gave me that look. My heart skipped a beat as embarrassment washed over my body and I suddenly began to sweat. Having a darker skin tone tends to hide any visible signs of embarrassment or else those in the room would have seen red splotches start to appear on my neck as my internal temperature shot through the roof. If I could have visibly "turned red," I would have.

The president looked at me with his head cocked to one side, then his chair, then back at me with a slight smile. He probably thought he was getting punked! I popped up like a cork just unleashed from a champagne bottle and let forth a volley of apologies for sitting in the wrong seat. Talk about wrong place–wrong time! The president's response was classic. Mr. Bush just chuckled and gave me this quizzical look that said, *What the heck are you doin' in my chair, bud?* I apologized again and he dismissed it immediately, "Don't worry about it. I'm not staying. I was just stopping by."

Then he gave me that look again, which of course initiated a fresh round of *mea culpas*. He was more reassuring the next time. "Really. It's OK. Don't worry about it, man." He then paused and said, "It's just the president's chair."

The aides in the room burst into laughter. The president started laughing as well. I didn't know whether to nervously laugh along or apologize again. The only thing I was sure of was that I wanted to disappear. Before the president turned on his heels towards his office in the front of the plane he said with a twinkle in his eye, "I'm just giving you a hard time, man. Don't worry about it."

I forgot about the rest of my briefing and retreated back to the junior staff cabin, still hot with embarrassment, but relieved the president had taken my grotesque breach of protocol in stride and with a bit of levity.

Visit to Hallmark Cards Inc.
When you care enough to
send the very best!

The next morning, February 1, 2008, the president toured Hallmark Cards Inc. As part of his tour he stopped by Kaleidoscope, an interactive learning center for elementary school children to participate in art lessons and creative projects. The purpose: personal enrichment and self-expression. I had been there before – 20 years prior on a school field trip. If someone had told me when I was eight that 20 years later I would return to Kaleidoscope, the site of my elementary school field trip, with a sitting head of state, I probably would have scratched my head in bewilderment. The significance of the moment wasn't lost on me. *The native son returns home*, I thought.

Kaleidoscope was a whirlwind of activity. Some children from Horizon Elementary School in Shawnee, Kansas ran around the facility laughing and screaming with delight, lost in a cloud of multi-colored construction paper, glitter, and crowns. It was a comical picture when combined with the ever-serious, gun-toting Secret Service. Could these harmless little children really be a threat to the president? The president zeroed in on a corner of the room where about ten kindergarten students were seated around a table. He took a seat in an undersized chair and struck up a conversation. After finding out they were making handcrafted letters and cards to military personnel serving in Iraq, he sat down to join in their project.

My Best Day – Our Best Moment

The last event before heading back to D.C. took us north from downtown Kansas City to Parkville, Missouri in support of Congressman Sam Graves' re-election. At the time, his re-election bid was too close to call. Former Kansas City Mayor Kay Barnes was widely popular, and political indicators pointed towards a difficult re-election battle. We were hoping a visit from the president could help Graves raise some needed cash to remain viable against a strong and worthy opponent. As the motorcade neared the residence of businessman Robert Wilson and his wife Twyla, it seemed odd that the presidential entourage could invade and take over a small Midwestern neighborhood, but it did. As our 20-vehicle motorcade turned off the highway and into Parkville, the entire town seemed to stop and watch the procession.

The motorcade came to a halt at the Wilson's residence. As the president and entourage of White House staff and Secret Service all filed out, I went in search of some very special guests for the fundraiser, Mom and Dad. My parents could never afford to attend a fundraising event like this. They would have needed thousands of dollars to gain entry on their own, but Jason Recher saved the day again. He asked me a few days before the trip began if my parents were going to attend the fundraiser. I told him they couldn't afford it, but he insisted I invite them as guests of the White House and the president.

"You helped plan this entire three-day trip. Of course you should invite your parents. Don't give it a second thought. Oh, and put them in the photo op line to take a picture with the president. You earned it," was Jason's heartfelt directive.

I found my parents in the kitchen peering out the windows at Secret Service snipers and counter-assault agents stationed near the home and in the forest a few yards away. There was a sniper dressed all in black standing on the Wilson's deck with a large long-range caliber weapon peering through his scope and sweeping the perimeter for potential threats. Mom and Dad were intrigued by all the heavy artillery that went into protecting the president. I was glad to have found them in the mass of people. They were in a line waiting to take a photo with the president. I gave them a big hug and then proceeded to tell them not to embarrass me!

"Dad, straighten your tie. Mom, you look great; No your lipstick is not smudging. It's perfect; Yes. Your hair is perfect, too. Just don't embarrass me! PUH-LEASE."

I was mostly teasing – but kind of serious, too. If you've ever had a proud parent try and advocate on your behalf to your boss, you know what I mean. I gave them another hug and started to walk away when Recher and Jared Weinstein turned me around and pushed me back in the line towards them.

Recher said, "Introduce your parents to the president."

As I considered doing so my heart started beating a little bit faster as adrenaline coursed through my veins. On the other hand I felt a sense of pride to be able to introduce Mom and Dad to the president; especially Mom. She had done so much for me. It was her love and her sacrifice that had brought us to that moment.

My mind rushed to come up with the proper introduction as the line wound down and we were next. I stepped forward and at a loss for anything profound, intellectual or witty, simply said, "Mr. President, this is my mom and dad, Dorothy and Larry Boyce."

The president got this big smile on his face as he shook their hands. I wonder if he had ever considered that my parents were a different color than me. He had us all take a photo together and afterwards proceeded to drape his arms around Mom and Dad, pulling them in for a quick chat. He told my parents what a great job I had been doing for the country and how this was my first big trip across the United States with him.

He said, "Your son is doing a fantastic job for us and you should be proud of how he turned out. You did a great job in raising him."

Then he kind of gave me this sideways glance and a slight smile as he launched into the next part.

"The only thing about your son is…" the president let silence fill the room as he paused for effect. As he did so my palms became instantly sweaty and I couldn't breathe… Then he finished his line… "He likes to sit in my seat on Air Force One."

He along with my parents and the other White House staff present erupted in laughter. *Whew! Not a total disaster!* I thought. The president then briefly retold for my parents the events of the night before on the plane. My parents and he proceeded to laugh it up while I got this sheepish look on my face. The president gave me a wink as he said, "Just kiddin' ya."

> *Achieving goals doesn't amount to much if you can't share them with the ones in life that mean the most to you.*

I was worried that Mom would be the one to say something to embarrass me. I never thought it would be the president, and yet the moment of semi-embarrassment was an endearing one as well. I think of it often, because while the president made a joke at my expense, it was one of the most memorable and gratifying moments of my life. It was special but more so because I wasn't alone. It was our moment. I got to share it with my hero; with Mom. Achieving goals doesn't amount to much if you can't share them with the ones in life that mean the most to you. As I've touched on before, moms don't always get the accolades they deserve. I know this to be true for my mom especially. Like politicians or leaders in business, sometimes moms are often dismissed, unappreciated, second-guessed or all of the above. It doesn't matter whether it's friendly fire from the ones closest to them, or some Monday morning quarterback in society who thinks they can do it better. I'm blessed that my mom didn't give up even when the "haters" were showing their true colors. Her life example was a springboard for me and every other life she touched. And it was her life example that made a few hearty minutes with the leader of the free world, in a living room, at a fundraiser, one of our best moments together. The cherry on top was to hear her receive a little praise, not from me or Dad, but from the president.

For all of the exhilarating experiences that working at the White House can afford, my best day wasn't in the East Room or the Oval Office. Not the Capitol Rotunda or the South Lawn. Best days, more often than not, are not planned in advance. Most of the time best days come as a complete surprise. They will come when you least expect it. One thing is pretty certain. Our best moments will always come with those who mean the most. For all the dreams I set out to accomplish, my best day unfolded where it all began – at home. And my best moment took place with the most important person in my life – my mom. It was better than all my planning.

CHAPTER ELEVEN

WORLD CHAMPIONS ON AND OFF THE COURT

To be world champions on and off the court, delivering
legendary moments every step of the way.
—Orlando Magic Mission Statement

A Time of Transition

The summer and fall of 2007 brought me back down to earth. A highlight of the summer was flying aboard Air Force One, but the president's term was ending soon. It seemed like every few weeks a fellow colleague would send out a farewell email with forwarding contact information. As more and more White-House staffers began their exodus, I began to think about the next phase of my life and where it might lead. Everyone I asked from family to friends to professional colleagues seemed to have the same response. *You can do whatever you want now! You worked at the White House.*

Perspective employers would mention the same thing to me, but I wasn't quite convinced. I had never lived my life with an entitlement philosophy and wasn't about to start now. It was foolish to think that because I had worked at the White House, that now I was on easy street. In my experience life didn't work that way. We had a saying at the White House, "You're only as good as your last event."

There was no sense in resting on my laurels expecting anything just to be handed to me. Besides, Washington D.C. was full of "young suits" who had served at the White House, on the Hill or in previous administrations. I didn't see the advantage I had over a town full of political hacks and policy wonks.

I never intended to stay in D.C. after my term of service. I always thought that at the end of the road I would return home to Missouri to pursue the next goal on a smaller stage. I thought the prudent path for me was a law degree. At least that's what I thought. With most things in life, plans don't always unfold exactly how one would envision. And it was no less true for me. I began to study in earnest for the LSAT, determined to attend Washington University Law School in St. Louis. I had no idea that another chance encounter on the South Lawn of the White House would eventually propel me in a different direction. "Wait. I will show you something," was an ever-constant assurance.

Little League at the White House

July 15, 2007 brought little league baseball to the South Lawn of the White House. The president loved baseball and began a tradition of inviting little league teams to the White House to play each summer in 2001. The theme of this game was special because we honored Jackie Robinson and featured guests from the Negro leagues. Hall of Famer

Frank Robinson served as the commissioner for the game. I watched as he and the president "retired" Jackie Robinson's number 42 Dodger's jersey just like they did in many major league parks across the country that summer. It was a fitting honor for the famed star that broke the color barrier in professional baseball. Former major league players Tommy Lasorda, Don Newcombe, Clyde King, and Ralph Branca, who had the opportunity to play with Jackie, were there as well. Karl Ravech of ESPN served as commentator and my good friends Marc Morial, president of the Urban League, and Roslyn Brock, chairwoman of the NAACP, all came out to pay homage to Jackie Robinson and watch a little t-ball on the South Lawn. My only task for the day was to escort the artist Mario through the White House and get him to the appointed place to sing the national anthem before the first pitch.

Upon conclusion of the game and subsequent barbeque, I finished escorting Mario's entourage and said goodbye to Rosyln Brock and Marc Morial. I proceeded back to my office in the EEOB via the West Wing. I took the path up the driveway towards the South Portico of the White House. On my left was the expanse of a plush, perfectly manicured South Lawn where Marine One, the president's helicopter, typically sets down. To my right was a Secret Service post. Oblivious to the heavily armed man in full sniper gear, I was "alone" in reflection as I walked up the path toward the East Wing. *What's next?*, I thought. *It's going to be difficult to produce an experience quite like this.* I had just watched Tommy Lasorda umpire third base of a little league t-ball game in a tucked away corner of the South Lawn on a specially made baseball diamond in honor of Jackie Robinson. Self-doubt and uneasiness about the future began to creep into my mind. I wasn't completely sold on law school. I needed to be on the go – doing something, being busy, helping people, being part of something larger than myself. Sitting in a lecture hall, pouring over books for the next three years didn't seem like it fit the bill, at least not then. I pushed the thoughts of self-doubt away, convinced it was the "wise" choice. White House Communications Director Kevin Sullivan caught up with me and struck up a conversation. We talked about a variety of things and then he sprung the question of the day. "What's next for you after the Administration is over? Have you thought about what you will do when the term comes to an end?"

It seemed everywhere I turned someone was asking me the same question. I gave him the pre-recorded, canned response. "I'm studying for the LSAT and plan to go to law school back home in Missouri."

Then for some reason it just popped out. I don't know whether it was because we had just attended a sporting event or what. It wasn't top of mind, but I just blurted it out, "You know Kevin, to be honest. I've always wanted to work for an NBA team."

Kevin's response floored me. "I used to work for an NBA team. I was in charge of communications with the Dallas Mavericks."

"You've got to be kidding," I said. "Would you mentor me and help me explore the opportunity? I have no idea how to get a foot in the door with the industry. The only background I have in sports is as the professional sports liaison, but I'm unsure how that translates."

I'm thankful that Kevin said yes. Over the next month or two he sent me web sites and helped me research the industry. Never taking anything for granted is a big lesson I learned during the time I was outside of the White House looking in a few years before. So I continued my studies and the steady march to grad school, but kept the dream of working for an NBA team at the forefront of my mind.

A West Wing Tour Creates a Career Connection

I had never put real parameters on which NBA team I hoped to work for, especially since Michael Jordan wasn't playing anymore. It was a bit of providence that Kevin Sullivan was friends with a senior executive of the Orlando Magic organization. Early that September, after my first flight on Air Force One back from New Orleans, Kevin called me on the phone one weekday evening. "Would you be able to help me with a West Wing tour?" he asked.

West Wing tours were a big deal in the Bush Administration. You had to have the proper access to be able to give them in the first place and you could only take six at a time, because of the small, enclosed office spaces and walkways. Over the course of my time at the White House I can honestly say I had conducted hundreds and hundreds of tours for friends, colleagues, students, family, and key stakeholders of the Administration. It was always worthwhile, but over time you burn out after putting in a full 12-14 hour work day – and then spending the next two hours taking various people through. So in my head I said *Oh no. Another tour*, but my mouth said, "Sure, no problem."

I never wanted to be the person to say "no," and deny someone the opportunity to see what a special place the White House was. You never know who you might touch. I had witnessed several people cry after going through the tour. And no, it wasn't because I was a horrible tour guide. There was one instance when an individual stopped at the Oval Office and bowed their head to pray for the president. For all the tours and the time it took to give them, it was worth it to see people's eyes open wide when they see the Rose Garden for the first time, or step to the podium in the press briefing room. Without fail I would always hear, "Man, this looks a lot bigger on TV."

Kevin went on to explain who my guests would be that evening and it became clear: he was trying to give me a connection for the future. "My friend Joel Glass is in town on vacation with his family and friends. He is an executive with the NBA's Orlando Magic. I was hoping you could lead his tour."

I leapt at the chance. I met Joel Glass at the north entrance promptly at 7:00 p.m. and took him and his family through the West Wing. I didn't mention my ambition to work for an NBA team. I'm sure he'd heard it all before. My one goal was to give him a great tour and let the chips fall where they may. As the tour ended and we began to part ways, his wife Dolly, said, "Joel, tell him who you work for." I had an idea, but didn't let on. Joel was low key and demurred, but his children, Maddie and Max, were proud of their dad. With the White House lit up behind us as dusk settled in, they spent a few minutes excitedly telling me about their dad's work for the Magic. We exchanged businesses cards and I wished him well. The next day I sent my resume to Kevin who forwarded it on to Joel for consideration.

Joel's take on his family vacation in Washington D.C. came from a different perspective.

I remember walking up to the guard gate at 1600 Pennsyl-vania Avenue for what would turn out to be the highlight of our family vacation to Washington D.C. I knew how special this opportunity was and wanted to take it all in. The Secret Service and armed military guards at the front of the White House only punctuated the moment. We had planned the trip for some time and I had reached out to Kevin Sullivan, the former Dallas Mavericks PR director who was working in the Bush Administration, for some possible behind-the-scenes access. Kevin worked out the necessary security clearances prior to our arrival, but I was told to phone him when I arrived that evening. As you can imagine I was still a little uneasy if we would actually see more than the standard public tour. I phoned Kevin and learned he was tied up with obviously a more pressing matter. He said that he would send out a staffer to conduct our tour.

Lucas met us out front. I couldn't put a finger on it, but there was something about him from the moment we began our tour. He seemed down-to-earth, incredibly bright and knowledgeable, had a sense of humor, and was resourceful. We were standing in the Rose Garden and he was telling us about all the perks and amenities the president had at his disposal. He mentioned that the president had a basketball court. My six year old, Maddie, who was tiring from the long day, quipped back, 'Well, we have a basketball court.' As we tried to shush her, Lucas seemed to enjoy the moment.

Later, he asked if we wanted a family photo to commemorate the moment. I had told my wife and the other family travelling with us that there were no cameras allowed. As it turned out, there were cameras allowed. Lucas dashed off to find a camera to save the day, and me. For some reason, at this moment I remembered sitting in a senior leadership meeting at the Magic talking about how as an organization we always needed to be on the lookout for talent. Shortly after leaving the White House I sent a message to Lorisse Garcia, our chief recruiter at the Magic, saying we needed to hire Lucas. "I don't know what job we have open, or what the fit is, but we need to hire this kid."

Later that month, Lorisse Garcia phoned me to conduct an informational interview. There wasn't a good fit at that time, but I was so appreciative they would even reach out. It made me want to work for the Magic even more. Ms. Garcia offered advice on professional development and a few tips on how I should change my resume. She asked if the Magic could reach out if future opportunities presented themselves. I thought that was a gracious way of saying, "Thanks but no thanks – not what we're looking for!"

A few weeks later, I was promoted to the Office of Political Affairs where I received the opportunity, under the leadership of Jonathan Felts, to monitor political activity and track key races across the Plains-Southwest region of the United States. A huge blessing for me, the new position allowed me to coordinate communication, public relations and education outreach across diverse communities, constituencies and issues. I was completely happy with flying aboard Air Force One that one time on the flight back from New Orleans. I had fulfilled a dream and I didn't ever think the opportunity would come again. With the promotion, I found myself directing every trip the president took to my region of responsibility. This meant I would get to travel with him as well. I was reminded once again, "Wait, I will show you something." He did and it was better than all my planning.

New Department Provides Opportunity

I learned early on that the Orlando Magic's efforts in the community are a by-product of the team's mission, "To be world champions on and off the court delivering legendary moments every step of the way." When it came to the off-the-court component, president of the team Alex Martins saw the need for an enhanced strategy. Martins saw an emerging diversity in the Central Florida region. He believed the Magic organization could go from "good to great" and that in order to do so the organization would need to take some bold new steps rarely seen in the sports industry.

He believed to his core that as a leader in the community the Orlando Magic has the moral obligation to be everyone's team. So in the summer of 2008 he, along with Vice President of Community and Government Affairs Linda Landman Gonzalez, created a new department designed to respond to the needs, expectations, desires, and motivations of the multicultural residents who live and work in Central Florida. I remember exactly where I was when I heard about this new initiative. It was late March of 2008. I was walking back to the White House along Pennsylvania Avenue on a return trip from Starbucks when my phone buzzed. I pulled my blackberry out of its holster and opened an email from Lorisse Garcia. It took me a few moments to recognize who the sender was. *Lorisse Garcia. Who is Lorisse Garcia?* It had been almost eight months since we'd last spoken. She hadn't forgotten about me after all.

Faced with a changing landscape of multicultural diversity, the organization was seeking to reach out and be more inclusive of the entire community. Linda and her team were recruiting a champion for the effort and Lorisse was inquiring whether I might be interested in going through the process to determine whether I might be a good fit.

Lorisse told me the goal of this new department was to create an inclusive environment where community partners, fans and employees feel welcome, valued, and appreciated. This new initiative wouldn't be about political correctness, but about perspective and insight into the audiences the Magic wishes to reach and include in its business. Alex, Linda and the rest of the leadership team understood that working together through many different voices, backgrounds and cultures was their greatest opportunity for lasting success. Having served as the White House's liaison to the African American community, I understood what the Magic was trying to achieve and I was eager to take on the challenge and pursue the opportunity.

As I prepared to try and achieve an important life goal, I learned the Orlando Magic was owned by Rich DeVos, co-founder of Amway. The DeVos name was synonymous with family, faith, and philanthropy. It wasn't just his incredible life story of starting a venture in his garage with his friend Jay Van Andel and taking it to a billion dollar worldwide enterprise that was impressive. It was what he did with his success that President Bush and the rest of us most admired. We knew him as a man of ardent faith, incredible courage, and unwavering conviction. He was a man I wanted to work for and I was excited at the prospect of working for an organization with him at the helm. This was a team that walks the talk and I wanted desperately to join their ranks.

Orlando Bound

After finishing another cross-country trip with the president a few days prior, I flew to Orlando on June 4, 2008, in exhaustion, for the final phase of the interview process. I had never had to prepare a presentation for a seven-person panel interview before and was feeling a little trepidation. Pulling up to the RDV Athletic Club and taking in the expansive complex intimidated me even more. I walked through the lobby en route to the Magic corporate offices and passed by a window overlooking an Olympic sized swimming pool. I then crossed over a walkway overlooking an expansive fitness floor with floor to ceiling glass windows looking out towards six tennis courts. *What is this place?* I wondered. *This is an even bigger deal than I imagined.* The facility served as a practice facility for the players, athletic club for the community and Magic corporate offices all rolled up into one 365,000 square foot building taking up a full city block. I left a few hours later after having given the interview all I had. I was going to let the chips fall where they may. Worst case scenario I'd serve out the president's term and figure out what was next. After all, I still had law school I could fall back on.

The answer to what was next came two weeks later. I had just left my buddy Paris Dennard's office in the East Wing when my blackberry registered its familiar buzz. The area code on the caller ID was 407. Not sure who it was, I answered to hear the cheerful voice of Lorisse Garcia on the other end. *This was it*, I thought. *Do or die*. She was calling to ask me to join the team. I stopped in my tracks along the East Colonnade that overlooks the First Lady's Garden to fully take it in.

Getting a job with an NBA team is never a sure thing, even with White House service on your resume. There are only 30 NBA teams and, like national service to the federal government, I understood that to work for one of them was a unique and rare opportunity only experienced by a few. There were a number of exceptional and qualified candidates and I didn't believe in taking anything for granted. The only thing I knew is that win or lose, I would bow my head in thanksgiving and praise to God for the opportunity to just be considered and go through the process.

The ground floor of the White House features a large central hall lined with red carpet, vaulted ceilings, and mini chandeliers. As I walked along the ornate hallway, decorated with pictures of former first ladies, towards the West Wing, I couldn't concentrate. My heart filled with emotion as I passed by the China Room and the Diplomatic Reception Room. When I reached the West Wing Colonnade, I looked beyond the Rose Garden to the Oval Office, paused and bowed my head. Everything was about to change. I was moving to Orlando.

A Different Kind of NBA Team

There is no better place to work than one in which you get up every day knowing your efforts go toward a just cause and making a positive impact. I learned from my friend Chuck Perry that our life's ambitions should not be directed towards vocational success alone. There is more to life than that, something more meaningful. He said our lives should be organized around "being part of something that's not only vocationally successful but humanly significant."

Chuck's words became the standard by which I measure whether an endeavor is worthwhile. I never imagined I'd be able to fulfill both of those principles in working for an NBA team until I learned what the Magic was about beyond the noise of squeaking basketball shoes on the signature parquet floor.

On an annual basis the Orlando Magic gives more than $2 million to the local community by way of event sponsorships, donated tickets, autographed merchandise, scholarships and grants. Our foundation, the Orlando Magic Youth Foundation (OMYF), focuses on helping children in Central Florida realize their full potential, especially those most at risk. Since its inception, over $16 million has been granted through OMYF to local nonprofit organizations. Every year, approximately 75,000 kids are impacted through community initiatives. Orlando Magic employees volunteer over 5,000 hours in the community on an annual basis. Our Chairman Rich DeVos committed to build five recreation centers across Orange County. We hope they will provide even more opportunities for our community's youth.

Now, being familiar with the world of politics, I'm aware of the cynicism that tends to take root when someone discusses "giving back." I've fallen victim to "rolling of the eyes syndrome" as well. It happens in a world where most seem to have an ulterior motive even for doing good. It's unfortunate – even more so because we become desensitized to the leaders, organizations, and ordinary people who really strive to make a difference. When the Magic says "we care about our community" it's not just a catchy slogan. While winning basketball games is important, the difference we can make in the lives of our youth, or the unifying force we can provide to our community through the game of basketball, is of equal, and sometimes greater, value. Everyone in our organization, from our owners and leadership to our interns, understands what's possible and the role each of us has to play in building up our community. Whether it's driving our efforts to be an inclusive organization, overseeing our philanthropy efforts, or managing our government relations strategy, our job is simple: to ensure the organization walks the talk and makes an enduring, positive impact on Central Florida.

Dr. Martin Luther King Jr. described why we do this best when he said, "Whatever affects one directly, affects all indirectly. I can never be what I ought to be until you are what you ought to be."

The Magic believes the same thing. It's an organization where success is not measured alone by the number of Dwight Howard dunks on a given night, or the barrage of three pointers by J.J. Reddick and the score atop the Jumbotron at the end of each game. This organization has a depth of commitment to others unheard of in most professional sports teams. I remain in awe of the complete compassion, in terms of treasure and time.

Legendary Moments

It was two months after my 29th birthday when I joined the Orlando Magic. In only a short time, I've witnessed some legendary moments that have confirmed why this is one of the best teams in professional sports. With the economy in recession the Magic could have justified withdrawal from the community. I'm blessed to be part of a "family" who didn't flinch or waiver from their commitment to be a good neighbor, even when times are tough.

Thanksgiving at the Coalition for the Homeless

One of those moments was Thanksgiving 2008. Each year Magic employees including our mascot, Stuff, coaches, players, the dancers and former players Nick Anderson and Bo Outlaw visit the Coalition for the Homeless on Thanksgiving morning to serve breakfast to those most in need. Our entire organization joins in the effort to give a hearty meal, provide face painting, games, and activities in a carnival-like atmosphere to hundreds of homeless men, women and families. Before joining the Magic, I'd never thought to give thanks by giving back in quite this way and I was amazed at what I saw. The stereotypical image of the homeless is confined to men. But as I served trays of food to single mothers with children as young as three weeks, and as old as middle school, my heart broke.

I distributed bags of popcorn to young and middle aged men and in my mind wondered when they would eat again. I hid my concern and concentrated on providing a good time for those we served. I wanted them to smile and forget the toils of life, even if only for a few hours. I was consoled by the fact that our service wasn't just a flash in the pan. The Magic would be back and our employees would continue to give of themselves in volunteering their time and energy whenever they could. *It's not just lip service*, I thought. Here we were on Thanksgiving morning, trying to brighten the day for our community's most needy. It was one of the legendary moments our organization seeks. The goal, however, is not just a moment in time, but an enduring mark of our corporate culture.

Naturalization Ceremony at a Magic Game

Another legendary moment took place on Friday, October 23, 2009, during halftime at one of our pre-season games. It was a scorching hot day in Central Florida, but it didn't deter 81 people from 34 different countries coming to Amway Arena and taking their final steps to become U.S. citizens. As a way to further our commitment to the rich multicultural heritage of the Central Florida community, the Magic partnered with the Department of Homeland Security to host a naturalization ceremony. Our goal was to assist the federal government in securing America's promise as a nation of immigrants. During an afternoon ceremony we joined the candidates in singing our national anthem, received words of encouragement from Community Ambassador and former Magic player Nick Anderson and heard words of inspiration from President Barack Obama via videotaped message. Vice President of Community Relations and Government Affairs Linda Landman Gonzalez shared a few words with the candidates as well. She said, "As you cross over and become citizens of this country the call is, by your example, by your passion, assist in the work of our nation to become more inclusive and more welcoming to all. We need each individual and it will take a full team effort to be successful as a community, as a region and as a country."

> *We need each individual and it will take a full team effort to be successful as a community, as a region and as a country*
>
> **—Linda Landman Gonzalez,**
> Vice President, Community Relations and Government Affairs, Orlando Magic

Later that evening during a halftime ceremony, the applicants for naturalization fulfilled the oath of allegiance in front of a sold out crowd of over 17,000 fans. As they raised their right hands, some cried while others excitedly waved mini American flags. Our fans stood as one and put their hands to their hearts as three of the newest citizens, who were members of the armed forces, led the Pledge of Allegiance for all.

The moment wasn't lost on the new citizens either. Orlando Magic staffer Noah Sharfman caught up with a few of the applicants for citizenship and recorded their feelings of what the moment meant to them.

Kiran and Manjula Babaladi, husband and wife from India, had waited more than ten years to become citizens of the United States. Once the wait was over, their first few moments as U.S. citizens could be described as nothing short of simply magical. "It's very emotional actually," Manjula Babaladi said. "I'm proud to be a U.S. citizen, because this has given me my livelihood here and it's given me a privilege to be independent and be whatever I want." For Kiran Babaladi the Magic played a large role in one of his proudest days. "I've been to Magic games before," Kiran Babaladi said, "but to be on the court; amazing."

Among the 81 candidates for citizenship were three active members of the U.S. Armed Forces. Jose Salazar of the U.S. Army came to America about nine years ago with the hopes of accomplishing his life goals. "Now that I'm a citizen it feels good to say it, because now I can go through and complete my dreams," Salazar said. "I'm going to be an officer for the R.O.T.C. and then I'm going to serve my country. I'm very proud to be a citizen now of the United States and I'm really going to be thankful and pay this return to serving this country." For Salazar, joining the Army prior to becoming a U.S. citizen was a way to give back to the country that gave him so much. "To be in this country has brought me a lot of self-esteem and happiness with my family and everything," Salazar said. "[Joining the Army] was a reason to pay back this country just by serving it. I really love this country and I will fight for it and I'm willing to give my life for anything that will protect it. I'm very proud to be a citizen. It feels great to be saying that I'm a citizen of the United States of America."

I've been blessed to be part of some special moments over the years, but standing at center court and looking up into the bowl of the arena as our fans exploded with applause was electric. *God Bless the U.S.A* by Lee Greenwood played over the arena's speakers, and the fans joined along. It was a moment that left a lasting impression. And it was a defining moment for our Magic family. We were fulfilling a portion of our mission statement, to create legendary moments every step of the way on our journey to a championship.

On Being a Champion

While we haven't yet reached our goal to be world champions on the court, I've been blessed to be part of a premier basketball team that is doing their best to unite a community. We are happy to have accomplished so much, but as our patriarch Rich DeVos has said, "We are happy, but we are not satisfied. We have a ways to go."

Throughout our 2008-2009 playoff- run to the NBA finals, our President of Basketball Operations, Otis Smith, had a picture of the Larry O'Brien Championship Trophy on his door, a constant reminder of our goal. Once our season was complete, I walked by one day to see a simple message written on the poster. "Winning is selfless." The message rang through loud and clear for me. Whether on the court or off, if we are to be truly successful, we must be willing to give every ounce of ourselves to the goal we seek. So in order to win at the game of life, to be truly successful in business, or personal endeavors – sometimes we have to be willing to give up a little of what we want for the good of the whole. Everyone has a part to play in the journey.

> ### *Winning is selfless.*
> **—Otis Smith**
>
> President of Basketball
> Operations, Orlando Magic

We are happy with our team's success, but we are not yet satisfied. A great deal of work remains. As we began our 2009-2010 season, Otis shared with us an important principle that drove home the point that we must be selfless in order to be successful. His motto: "Everyone grab a handle." Each of us through our individual gifts must do our part. No more. No less.

Framed in hallways throughout the Magic's corporate offices is a visible reminder of what it means to be a champion. We read this creed collectively as an organization. It's posted on our walls and stored on our computers, because we embrace it in every aspect of our lives. I think we are able to embrace our mission because what it means to be a champion on the basketball court translates seamlessly into what it means to be a champion on the basketball court of life.

Orlando Magic President Alex Martins crystallized this sentiment in a few statements. He instills in us these principles on a consistent basis. He tells us that:

The momentum we feel is real and it is being spurred on – not just by the talent of our players – but by the talent of all our people. In our business, however, momentum is nothing if it is not propelling us towards one thing: becoming a champion. Certainly, this idea includes success on the basketball court, but it doesn't start or end there. In order for the Orlando Magic to be considered a true champion – to become an international icon of excellence – every member of the organization must act like a champion in every situation, in everything we do. This is not negotiable. We are a team, a single unit. And our focus on excellence must hold fast even when reduced to the least common denominator. Being a champion requires resolute commitment, and unwavering dedication. You're either in or you're out. There is no place for uncertainty. And the effort you give is returned tenfold by what you get back.

We all want to be successful and we all want to accomplish the dreams set before us. I'm thankful Alex's words are not exclusive to the Magic or even those involved in sports. His words have value and provide encouragement for everyone in every industry, endeavor, or phase of life.

Basketball, More than Just a Game

Basketball. It's just a game right? You pass. You Shoot. You score. It's simple… right? Then why all the drama, the glitz, and the fuss? Why all the expectations on players and NBA franchises to be "role models?" Aren't parents supposed to do that? Some argue that it shouldn't matter what a player does off the court, what he says, how he is perceived, what he tweets about, how he treats his fans or even the community's perception of his character. After all, it's just a game. The players are human beings. Heck, in a lot of cases, they are kids themselves.

I understand the desire of some who argue the *laissez faire* approach to the pressures of the game. I appreciate that point of view and I'd agree with it if it weren't for the powerful impact and influence of basketball in general and the NBA in particular, has had on the world. I can attest to its influence because of the NBA's impact as my model for motivation when barely a teenager. And if it made a difference in the life of a skinny and insecure 12 year old from Independence, Missouri, imagine how it can shape the lives, young and old, of millions around the globe.

Take this for example: who would have guessed the NBA could help a young boy with an anxiety disorder called "selective mutism" get excited about talking? Journalists Miriam Greenfield and Sabrina Peduto with ABC along with Rachel Nichols of ESPN first reported this remarkable story. It aired on ABC's *World News Now*, *Good Morning America* and even *World News* with Charles Gibson. The story demonstrates the incredible power of basketball and how this simple sport literally transformed the life of a young boy living in Orlando, Florida. At four years old, Ryan Rodriguez had never spoken more than a few words. Other children his age talked all the time displaying the typical chatter box curiosity of a toddler. Not Ryan though. He was quiet and withdrawn. He wouldn't engage anyone, not with his teacher, not even with his parents Izzy and Karen Hernandez.

It was during an NBA game on television one evening in March of that year when a breakthrough occurred. Izzy was watching an Orlando Magic game when something unexpected took place. ABC explains the moment best, "Ryan found his voice." "Ryan started pointing at the T.V.," his father said. "He sat there and kept going, 'Me, me, play, play." He'd never seen his son so excited and wanted to do something

– anything to keep the momentum going. So Mr. Hernandez did something he said was absolutely crazy. He purchased an expensive pair of playoff tickets to take his son to an NBA game hoping the tiny spark stirred inside his son would ignite to be something better. It was a courageous decision for a family on a budget with a monthly mortgage. Izzy and Karen's great gamble paid off though – in dividends. The end result was "better than all their planning."

On April 28, 2009, Izzy took Ryan to his first NBA game and this is what happened when they arrived in the well of the arena that evening. "When we get there, he says, 'Me, play basketball, here?'" Rodriguez said. "So I look down and dropped to my knees and said 'What did you say?' He said, 'Me play basketball here?' I said, Yeah." Izzy says Ryan and he kept talking throughout the entire game. It was an amazing breakthrough. "I'm thinking, OK, I'm dreaming. Or something happened, or maybe this is what he needed. [He] talked to me all the way home," Rodriguez said. "I talked to Karen on the cell phone crying all the way home."

The story doesn't end there however. The next day, Mr. Rodriguez wrote an e-mail to the front office staff for the Orlando Magic. "I just can't believe what an impact you all had on my son. I just want to say thank you from the bottom of my heart for the most priceless moment in my life, hearing Ryan talk," the message read. The email reached Joel Glass, Orlando Magic Vice President for Communications who took immediate action to try and help the family even more. Joel made sure the family was given tickets throughout the remainder of the playoffs that year at no cost to the Rodriguez family. Ryan's parents said he opened up in ways they had never dreamed of. "It's priceless," Rodriguez said. "You can't ask for more. And those guys who play, the whole organization, and I know a lot of teams… do a lot of stuff for children, but being that close to a miracle is priceless."

Basketball began as an idea to keep students entertained indoors during the winter months of 1891 in Springfield, Massachusetts. Dr. James Naismith invented a sport he couldn't possibly know at the time would have the worldwide reach it does today. Think about it. The game started with just 13 rules, a soccer ball and two peach baskets for hoops. "Better than all his planning" I'm sure. Today the sport has literally grown into a global phenomenon. Its exponential growth and influence is akin to a small and seemingly insignificant snowball that gathers momentum to become an avalanche. Compare basketball's humble beginnings, 119 years ago, to its domestic impact and international influence today, and it's obvious the snowball has become an avalanche of opportunity poised to shape the world. The sport, another example that "necessity is the mother of invention," has become a dominant force that has brought the world closer together and forged common ground among the nations.

According to a Sports Intelligence 2008 Report, among 16-34 year olds globally, basketball is the top participation team sport with 28 percent, slightly ahead of soccer at 26 percent. Every year, the NBA Finals is the most popular annual sporting event among teens globally according to Teenage Research Unlimited 2009. The Sports Intelligence Report further reveals:

> *An estimated 300 million people play basketball in China and 96 percent of Chinese people ages 12-65 know of the NBA. The same source found the highest basketball participation rates internationally are in Asia but that Europe is also becoming more and more influenced by the NBA as well. There are 111.7 million NBA fans (very or somewhat interested in the NBA) in key European markets (Germany, France, UK, Italy, Spain, Greece, and Turkey). The sport has also enjoyed wide*

participation among the multicultural panacea that makes up the United States. According to Experian Simmons, U.S. Hispanics currently make up 16 percent of the total NBA fan base while 30 percent of U.S. Hispanics are considered NBA fans.

It doesn't stop there. Media is providing a platform to reach more and more living rooms and computers as well. According to NBA league reports, as of this writing, NBA T.V. is in more than 53 million homes across America. NBA.com currently receives more international traffic than any other U.S. based sports website. More than 50 percent of those visitors come from outside of North America. NBA games and programming will reach 215 countries and territories in more than 40 languages during the 2010-11 season.

But beyond its economic and cultural renaissance, the NBA is achieving something much more significant, which is why it can't be just a game. There was no way I could see it as a teenager looking up to Michael Jordan as he smashed through obstacles on his way to six world championships. It's been later in life that I've fully realized what the game offers each of us and how those lessons, if accepted, can shape countless lives.

Some think basketball is just a game, but whether we like it or not this simple sport is much more than that. The NBA's reach and influence bare this out. So if it's more than a game – then what is it? In my opinion the NBA is a platform to export the best virtues of our country and a model for social progress and personal development. So the corporate character of the different franchises and the individual choices and characters of the NBA's players does matter. Young people are watching and looking for examples to pattern their lives. And whether we like it or not, the examples they see and hear will serve as impressionable models for behavior. If you need more proof, look no further than Ryan Rodriguez and the catalyst that fueled his breakthrough in speech.

The NBA Cares "It's Just a Game" commercial, first seen on television during the 2009-2010 season, shows that the NBA and its players understand the inherent responsibility to, as my mom always says, "remember who they are and who they represent." In the commercial, a number of the NBA's greatest stars, Shaquille O'Neal, Kobe Bryant, Labron James, Steve Nash, Yao Ming, and Chris Paul team up with a cast of children to show us basketball is more than just a game. The commercial alternates between the players and a multicultural mix of young children who explain what basketball means to them and what it can teach all of us if we are willing to listen. If you've ever had the opportunity to view the commercial on television or on You Tube the message is clear. This "simple sport" has some incredible wisdom to offer us as we go about our daily lives. That basketball is about patience, unity, sacrifice, love, confidence, and team work are the driving themes of this short video montage. A few moments stand out but at one point during the 60 second spot Kobe Bryant tells us:

> Basketball brings us together," followed up by a young girl, "It connects us." "We dream bigger. We dream higher," a duo of middle schoolers say. "Sometimes we win. Sometimes we don't. [on the court and in life.] But no matter what we always have to work hard. Basketball teaches that even when there's no chance to win. There's still an opportunity to be a hero." And if we can practice all those things to make our game better? Can't we practice all those things to make our world better?

It's not just children, though, who are impressionable and need role models to look up to for inspiration. Older adults gather strength and catch inspiration from this sport and its players as well. First reported in the *Orlando Sentinel* by Mike Bianci, is the story of a 62 year-old woman with terminal cancer whose one wish was to hang out with NBA All Star center Dwight Howard. Kay Kellogg, who has Stage 3 Multiple Myeloma said this about the Magic star:

> *Dwight Howard is just such a precious, wonderful kid. Whenever I watch him play, he just makes me feel good inside. That's a big statement as Bianci reports, considering the battle with chemotherapy that is raging inside of Kay. Kay was once a graceful and athletic ballet dancer. Now her battle with cancer relegates her to a walker. Back in September 2010 Kay's daughter, Arian Clute, wanted to lift her mother's spirits so she took a chance and contacted team officials about her mother's condition with a wish. Dwight showed up on her doorstep a few days later and spent over two hours hanging out at her home. "He has become my 7-foot-tall bottle of medicine," Kay said. Dwight asked Kay why he was the only one on her bucket list to which she replied, "Because some people get a choir that sings them into heaven and some people get a chariot that rolls them into heaven. Not me. I want to be slam-dunked – smack, dab into the middle of heaven by Dwight Howard.*

Dwight Howard views the responsibility of players to be role models this way:

> *Playing in the NBA has allowed us to help people all over the world. That's why we play basketball. To bring joy into people's*

lives and we also need to do that off the court. Just to see the impact that we as NBA Players have is bigger than basketball. We have an ability to touch people's lives wherever they might be. That's why I smile so much.

The NBA.

Basketball.

It's people like Ryan and circumstances like Kay's, and players with character like Dwight that prove … it's more than just a game.

<><><><><><><><><><><><><><><><><><><><><><><><><><><><><>

*When our hard work, determination and opportunity
meet with grace – anything can happen.*
—Lucas Daniel Boyce

*But God who loves little trees whispered to him, "wait I
will show you something." And He did. In all my dreams
I never thought [it] would turn out like this. I'm part
of a miracle. This is better than all my planning.*
—Taken From *Better than all Your Planning*

You Can Be Living Proof

I know you desire to reach beyond the current circumstance and achieve all that this world can offer. If you're willing to take a leap and practice the key principles I've shared, you too can be living proof that goals are realized, dreams come true and people of character really do finish first. The choice is yours. What's next for you? If the possibilities were endless and there were no limits to what you could achieve, what would you pursue? What would you dream? Go for it! Why not now?

We may have different experiences, circumstances, obstacles, challenges and goals. Regardless of who you are, where you come from and where you want to go, each of us has a decision to make. You can choose to stand still and do nothing or you can actively take the step forward and reach for something more. You don't need a great deal of money. You don't need celebrity, fame, or family connections. Your home life doesn't have to cripple you and neither does your height,

weight or "worldly smarts." We all need help and I'm not suggest-
ing you can be what you want to be on your own. I'm living proof
that it takes a loving support system, hard work, potential setbacks
and incredible grace; but I'm more interested in what you can prove.
It might play out differently. Your goals and dreams will be different
from mine. Your obstacles and seeming limitations may be shared, or
altogether different, but our stories can be the same and the end result
can be better than all your planning.

"Give Me a Place to Stand," Said Archimedes, "And I Can Move the World."

The cynics among us tear down our dreams and would have us
look to the future with fear and doubt. But the call of our generation,
young and old, is to not let what's possible fade with disbelief. Our
great responsibility is to pick up the torch of progress, the torch of
service and run with patience the race that is set before us.

You may think the calling is too big, the job too hard, or the way
too fearful... Before you make that conclusion, consider these words
from Robert F. Kennedy:

> Some believe there is nothing one man or one woman can do
> against the enormous array of the world's ills – against misery,
> against ignorance, or injustice and violence. Yet many of the
> world's great movements, of thought and action, have flowed
> from the work of a single man [or woman]. A young monk
> began the protestant reformation, a young general extended
> an empire from Macedonia to the borders of the earth, and a
> young woman reclaimed the territory of France. It was a young
> Italian explorer who discovered the New World, and 32 year

old Thomas Jefferson who proclaimed that all men are created equal. "Give me a place to stand," said Archimedes, "and I will move the world." These men moved the world, and so can we all.

Now is the time to move the world and why not you be the one to move it? Now is the time to dream big, step forward and lead. Why not this place to begin? Because who knows? God could be trying to show you something. And it could be better than all your planning.

I shared RFK's statement and those words with some middle school students at Lake Nona Middle School in November 2010. The students' response confirmed one of my greatest hopes, that a powerful generation is growing up before us and destroying a myriad of obstacles in the process. Mrs. Tiana Reyes, who was in charge of the school's AVID Program, called me to come and speak.

AVID stands for Advancement Via Individual Determination and is a college-readiness program designed to increase the number of students who enroll in four-year colleges. AVID serves all students, but focuses on the students who would be considered "average." More than half of AVID students are Latino, 17 percent are African-American, and 67 percent are eligible for free or reduced lunch programs. Many AVID students will be the first in their families to continue their education and go on to college. The AVID program began in 1980 when Mary Catherine Swanson created the initiative to help her English class at Clairemont High School in San Diego, California. Since then, AVID has been taught in nearly 4,500 schools in 47 states, 16 countries, and serves approximately 400,000 students.

Mrs. Reyes, along with a host of other AVID teachers, believes in this simple formula, "raise expectations of students and, with the AVID support system in place, they will rise to the challenge." The children are meeting the challenge. So far 90 percent of AVID graduates go onto college. In many cases the students had backgrounds similar to my own; they were struggling in school and needed to know that if they were willing to put forth the effort they could be living proof too.

I shared with 60 seventh and eighth graders from the school's Avid program what it takes to accomplish your goals and told them that they are built to succeed. I referenced Sam and Mac Anderson Parker's book *212 Degrees: The Extra Degree,* which explains the exact temperature required to make water boil. At 211 degrees water is just hot. It's only at 212 degrees that it has the power to make a difference. I shared with the students that this extra degree of effort is what would set them apart from the crowd and help them blossom into the individuals they were meant to be. I shared with the students the story you've just read about an illegitimate mistake with failure as my birthright who was able to overcome the cards life dealt and accomplish my goals. I shared with them that no matter what the circumstance, what their background or struggle, that my story could be their story as well. They can be living proof that setbacks can become stepping stones.

A few weeks later, just before Thanksgiving, I received a large envelope in the mail. In the envelope were cards and letters from the students expressing the impact our time together had on them, and that they were willing to embrace the moment and take action towards their life goals. It took me a full hour to read through all the letters and cards. Some of the notes were downright hilarious while others were deeply moving.

Here's what a few of the students said.

Taylor wrote: "You showed me that giving up is not an option and to always have hope. From now on I will work extra hard in school and improve myself."

Gabriella created an elaborate card that had inscriptions from some of the quotes from Dwight Howard, and Mom's two keys for success on the front. The inside left panel was a reminder of the encouragement I shared with the children, to live life at 212 degrees. Gabriella wrote, "At this level [212] anything is possible." She added a p.s. to her card, "After you told us about your life story and how you struggled, you have made my life goals seem so much more possible. Never give up!"

Nicholas wrote me and said, "Thank you for opening my eyes to see what I am capable of doing. I felt like I had a glow of courage. Thank you again for doing something for me that no one else could."

A note from another student named Gabriella especially moved me. Here is what she said:

The fact that you went through all that and still accomplished your goals made me feel like I can do that too. My mom has been diagnosed with breast cancer. She is treated with chemotherapy and God willing, she'll be done with her treatment on November 24th. Times have been tough, and at times, I feel like just giving up. But, since I heard your speech, I've been thinking about starting a really big breast cancer foundation. I'm thinking about raising money and sending it to the labs to try and find a cure. Unfortunately, I'm too young and I'm still in school. Yet, soon enough, I'll be out of school and ready to begin! I also want to be a photographer. I'd love to make a career out of it but I have no idea how to do so. And, once again, I now have the courage to continue my dream. All thanks to you.

Kaycee said, "Thank you so much for coming out and teaching us so many things. I will never give up. I will always be strong and never let anyone tell me that I can't do something cause I can if I put my mind to it."

Another student expressed how the speech gave her courage to "ignore the haters" and go after her dreams. She said she had more hope and she now understood that she and she alone has the power to control the outcome of her life.

As I read through the cards and letters I was reminded by RFK's words that the course of history could be altered and the world could be moved, if a person is willing to do whatever is necessary to make it so. RFK referred to conquerors like Alexander the Great, reformers like Martin Luther, explorers like Christopher Columbus, liberators like Joan of Arc, and young patriots like Thomas Jefferson.

I thought to myself how these students were following in the footsteps of trailblazers who have long since gone and that a new amazing generation is growing up before our very eyes. I was filled with emotion as I went over the notes from these students, confident that they, and many other young people like them in schools and universities all over the world are growing into future liberators, heroes, and champions.

"Give me a place to stand," said Archimedes, "and I will move the world."

The opportunity before us now is to do just that. I encourage you to commit to practice the principles you've learned, take the required action and go make an incredible impact on this generation. Don't yield to the voice of fear and allow the obstacles, real or imagined, to cause you to shrink from the opportunity of the moment and do nothing. Instead, set big goals, ask "why not?," follow the keys to lasting success, and achieve them. Contribute to the forward advance of this nation's social progress, and most importantly, in everything that you do, seek to leave the world a better place than you found it.

I'm certain, if you are willing to do your part, the end result *will be better than all your planning.*

> *Compelled to set aside each obstacle and every weight.*
>   *The opportunity is to run faster now – and to win this race.*
>
> *For your response, Heaven wonders and History, she waits.*
>   *Today. Right Now. In this moment. In this place.*
>
> *A generation is rising – with new tasks of leadership to embrace.*
>   *Because Now is the Time. And this is the Place.*

You can contact Lucas Daniel Boyce at:

Lucas Boyce
c/o Lucas Boyce Holdings Inc.
P.O. Box 540421
Orlando FL, 32804
Lucas@lucasdanielboyce.com

If you would like to have Lucas Boyce speak to your
school, group or organization, contact Wendy Kurtz at
BookLucas@WendyKurtz.com or call (407) 876-7730.

How can you use this book?

MOTIVATE

EDUCATE

THANK

INSPIRE

PROMOTE

CONNECT

Why have a custom version of *Living Proof?*

- Build personal bonds with customers, prospects, employees, donors, and key constituencies
- Develop a long-lasting reminder of your event, milestone, or celebration
- Provide a keepsake that inspires change in behavior and change in lives
- Deliver the ultimate "thank you" gift that remains on coffee tables and bookshelves
- Generate the "wow" factor

Books are thoughtful gifts that provide a genuine sentiment that other promotional items cannot express. They promote employee discussions and interaction, reinforce an event's meaning or location, and they make a lasting impression. Use your book to say "Thank You" and show people that you care.

Living Proof is available in bulk quantities and in customized versions at special discounts for corporate, institutional, and educational purposes. To learn more please contact our Special Sales team at:

1.866.775.1696 • sales@advantageww.com • www.AdvantageSpecialSales.com

LaVergne, TN USA
12 April 2011
223824LV00005B/56/P